# Ciao Italia
## *Slow and Easy*

ALSO BY MARY ANN ESPOSITO

*Ciao Italia Pronto!*

*Ciao Italia in Tuscany*

*Ciao Italia in Umbria*

*Ciao Italia: Bringing Italy Home*

*Ciao Italia*

*Nella Cucina*

*Celebrations Italian Style*

*What You Knead*

*Mangia Pasta!*

Mary Ann Esposito

# Ciao Italia
## *Slow and Easy*

Casseroles, Braises, Lasagne, and Stews from an Italian Kitchen

ST. MARTIN'S PRESS ❧ NEW YORK

www.stmartins.com
Design by Kathryn Parise

LIBRARY OF CONGRESS CATALOGING-IN-PUBLICATION DATA

Esposito, Mary Ann.
    Ciao Italia slow and easy  :  casseroles, braises, lasagne, and stews from an
Italian kitchen / Mary Ann Esposito.—1st ed.
        p.   cm.
    ISBN-13: 978-0-312-36292-8
    ISBN-10: 0-312-36292-7
  1. Casserole cookery.   2. One-dish meals.   3. Cookery, Italian.   I. Ciao Italia
(Television program)   II. Title.

TX693.E76   2007
641.8'21—dc22
                                                          2007028181


10  9  8  7  6  5  4  3

# CONTENTS

CONTENTS

# ACKNOWLEDGMENTS

This is my tenth cookbook and it seems each time that I write one, I am forever blessed with the expert help of so many people who bring the work to completion. To my editor, Michael Flamini, who is energy and enthusiasm personified, I wish to say thank you for not only your guidance, but for constantly stirring your spoon in a minestrone soup of ideas for today's home cook. And many thanks to all those I never get to see who work behind the scenes at St. Martin's Press, including Vicki Lame, Steve Snider, Courtney Fischer, Cheryl Mamaril, and Jane Liddle. Thanks to my agent, Michael Jones, Esq., who has developed his own unique cooking style over the years, and I'd like to think that it has been my books that have inspired him! To my husband, Guy, the beneficiary of all the recipes tested for this book, for his constructive criticism, patience, and love. To my daughter-in-law, Jennifer Chase Esposito, a wonderfully refreshing food writer (and excellent cook), for all her advice and reading of the manuscript. She is a stickler for punctuation! To Paul Lally, executive producer of *Ciao Italia*, the television series, for all his help with promotion of the book through our Web site, www.ciaoitalia.com, and for his endearing friendship. It continues to be a privilege to work with such a creative and extraordinary person. Thank you to the Dover Strategy Group for their marketing plan and strategies for promotion of the series and my cookbooks. Thank you to the underwriters of the series for their support and friendship: the Consorzio del Formaggio Parmigiano-Reggiano, and the Consorzio del Prosciutto di Parma, King Arthur Flour, Mohegan Sun, Winebow Inc., and Venda Ravioli. Thank you also to the National Italian American Foundation for their support, especially to Ken Ciongoli.

To those who had a hand in the design of this book, thanks go to book designer Kathryn Parise, to Dawn Smith for the beautiful photographs, and to Jeff Shaffer, who was a technical and creative force. To food stylist Frank Melodia and to Mamie Nashide for their artistic and fantastic eye in interpreting the recipes. To prop stylist Karen Quatsoe and to Elisha Ficalora at Vietri for the loan of beautiful cookware to show off the recipes as well as to Erica Sanborn at Home Goods for the generous loan of props. Thanks are not enough for Donna Petti Soares and Ruth Moore, cherished friends, and the most loyal culinary team that I have been blessed to have from the beginning. And to you, dear readers, my heartfelt thanks. Without you I could never have enjoyed such a journey. You always have a place at my table.

Acknowledgments

# INTRODUCTION
## The Art of the Well-Prepared Casserole

What is it that draws us to a bubbly, hot, and creamy, or crusty-topped casserole? Maybe it's the reminders of home and those old, familiar, cozy comfort foods that Mom used to make, the kind of food whose wafting smell welcomed and warmed us on a wintry day. Or maybe we're drawn to this food because we love casseroles for their ease of preparation and their versatility and compatibility with other foods, and because we can make them now and bake them later or freeze them. Or maybe because they are the perfect totable choice for a tailgate party or a potluck supper.

The word *casserole* has a complex history starting with the classical Greek term for cup *(kyathos)*, which progressed in Latin to *cattia*, meaning both a ladle and a pan, and eventually became the French word *casse*.

In Italian, *casseruòla* means pan. The Italian casserole evolved from the Renaissance days of sumptuary laws, issued by the Church, which forbade the serving of too many courses. To get around the law, many foods that would normally have been served separately were all mixed together.

One of the classic casseroles that comes to mind is a Tuscan dish, now almost lost to time, called *peposo* (page 38), a hearty stew of wild boar meat with a lot of pepper (from which the dish derives its name), pungent spices, and aromatic vegetables. It became the signature casserole of the town of Impruneta, an important tilemaking center, and while the tilemakers worked all day firing clay tiles, they stewed tough cuts of meat in earthenware pots and buried them in the hot embers of wood-burning ovens that were also used to bake bread. By the end of the workday, *peposo* was ready to eat. I like to think of this as the beginning of the "fix it and forget it" mantra.

For the purposes of this book, a casserole is a combination of ingredients, usually cooked together with some type of liquid or sauce. Or it can be a more structured, neatly layered affair with a variety of tastes and textures like a lasagne. Casseroles are usually assembled, cooked, and served in the same dish, which is part of their great appeal. In this book you will find classic Italian casseroles from various regions of Italy for today's busy cook that can either be prepared stovetop or oven baked. But before you begin to delve into the recipes, here are some pointers on how to ensure that your casseroles turn out *perfetto*! After all, there is more to a casserole than just throwing a bunch of ingredients into a pot.

1) The pan or pot should be one that can go from stovetop to oven to table and should be the right size for the amount of ingredients. When deciding what size to use, measure water into the pan before beginning the recipe and then dry it thoroughly. This will give you an accurate idea of how much it can hold. Pots and pans should be heavy ones that hold heat. I like to use enamel-coated cast iron, like Le Creuset, which requires no seasoning, or those old classic black cast iron pans that our grandmothers used and seasoned after each use with olive oil. They are also great at holding in heat. Holding in heat is critical to the final texture of a casserole. Copper is also good, although expensive, and hard to keep clean, but it is an excellent heat conductor. Heavy-gauge stainless steel pots like All-Clad are excellent

choices for casserole cooking because they can go from stovetop to oven.

For braising less tender cuts of meat like stew beef, shanks, and blade cuts, I use a 3½-quart braiser; for stews, a Dutch oven; for pasta and vegetable casseroles, a 12×8- or 14×10-inch rectangular glass or porcelain baking dish.

When I want a crust on a casserole, a shallower pan gives much better results than a deep one, which tends to make the top soggy. I do not recommend microwave cooking for any of these recipes because a casserole by its very nature needs time to meld the flavors, which will develop and intensify with slow, low-heat cooking.

2) Cut foods into uniform sizes and add those together that take about the same amount of time to cook; for instance, white potatoes, sweet potatoes, and carrots are hard vegetables, so they will cook well together, as opposed to combining zucchini chunks and potatoes—the more watery zucchini will cook much faster than the potatoes and turn to mush.

3) Use ingredients that complement, not fight, one another. For instance, for a fish casserole use mild-tasting herbs like parsley or thyme and use spices sparingly. For bold meat-based casseroles like beef or lamb use more intense-tasting herbs like oregano and tarragon. Rubs also work well in many casseroles. They can add depth of flavor, and so can toasting whole spices and grinding them in a spice mill before adding them to a dish. Little subtle changes in preparation can elevate a simple dish to sassy elegance.

4) For meat- and poultry-based casseroles, it is always best to sear and brown the meat pieces uniformly first over high heat on the stovetop before adding the rest of the ingredients. This will help to seal in the juices. And brown only a few pieces at a time; crowding the ingredients in the pan will result in steamed, not browned, meat or poultry, and there will be a loss of overall flavor.

5) The liquids used for casseroles can make all the difference in flavor. For braised casseroles, I lean toward wines, vegetable, beef, chicken, and fish stocks, beer, commercial balsamic vinegar, and cider. Water mixed with honey, mustard, or tomato juice can perk up flavor as well. For casseroles needing thicker sauces, make a standard white sauce (*besciamella*, page 97) ), using lowfat milk, butter or olive oil, and

flour. And of course, another standby for many casseroles is a zippy tomato sauce (page 99).

6) Salt according to taste; some dishes containing meats need rubbing before searing. All the recipes use sea salt, both fine and coarse unless otherwise noted, but how much to add is definitely a personal choice, so I have not indicated amounts of either. In Italian we say "*a piacere*," as you like.

7) Use fresh herbs and, if possible, add them at the end of the cooking time; this is easily done for stovetop casseroles. I usually add herbs about 2 minutes before the dish is ready, since adding them too soon will cause their oils to dissipate. For some casseroles, like the *timballo di maccarun* on page 64, it is necessary to add the herbs all at once because the dish is oven baked. As you experiment with the recipes, you be the judge of when you can add herbs at the right moment.

8) Some great casseroles come from what's on hand. Oftentimes leftovers can serve as the foundation for a great casserole like the ham and broccoli casserole on page 41.

9) Refrigerating a cooked casserole for the next day allows you to skim off any fat that has hardened, saving many calories.

10) Low heat cooking (between 275°F and 325°F) seems to work best for tough cuts of meat like veal shoulder, while 350°F is tops for pasta casseroles. Occasionally a dish such as the lamb and dandelion casserole on page 43 requires a higher temperature because of the soufflélike topping.

11) Use more grains like whole wheat berries and rice and less meat or poultry in a casserole as a filler.

12) To freeze a baked casserole, allow it to cool slightly, then wrap it tightly in heavy-duty aluminum foil. And here is a neat tip for freezing if you have only a limited number of casserole dishes: Line a casserole dish with heavy-duty aluminum foil and leave enough of an overhang so that you can cover the dish completely. Arrange the casserole ingredients in the lined pan and bake, cool, and freeze until solid; then lift the casserole from the pan, place it in a large Ziploc bag, label it, and freeze it. Do the same if you are preparing to freeze an unbaked casserole for later use, which you can then reposition in the casserole pan for baking at a later time.

**13)** For crispy-topped casseroles, do not cover them while they bake.

**14)** Make casseroles in pairs, one to bake now and one to freeze for later.

Casseroles never go out of style—they are ready when we are; they fit our lifestyle, and they always satisfy. So go ahead, try them all, whether for a good old-fashioned family supper or for guests. Casseroles rule!

# ITALIAN CHEESE WORLD

There are as many cheeses produced in Italy as there are types of pasta and wine. Some cheeses are just made for casseroles and those include good melting cheeses like Asiago, fontina, Gorgonzola dolce, Taleggio, mozzarella, scamorza, and young provolone. They not only combine and bind well in many casseroles but they also make great quick sauces.

Hard grating cheeses like Parmigiano-Reggiano, grana padano, and aged pecorino are great sprinkled on casseroles for a crusty top. When a spreadable cheese is needed, use fresh ricotta, either whole or skim.

Make sure you buy authentic Italian cheeses, not American processed varieties that are sold as Italian cheese. Italian cheeses have identifying marks or rinds. Always buy hard cheeses in wedges, not grated, to be sure that it is the real thing. There are many imitations sold.

When storing hard cheeses, keep them well wrapped in plastic wrap and placed in the warmest part of the refrigerator. Bring cheese to room temperature before using; hard cheeses such as pecorino or Parmigiano-Reggiano will grate better. Grate only as much cheese as is needed at one time. Re-wrap and store the rest. Softer cheeses such as mozzarella and Taleggio should be used as soon as possible to preserve their unique mild taste.

Get to know Italian cheeses because choosing the right cheese for the dish you are preparing will make all the difference. Here are some identifying characteristics of some of my favorite cheeses.

**Asiago,** recognizable by its brownish rind, is a cow's milk semi-firm cheese from the Veneto. Straw yellow in color with a rich nutty flavor, it is used as a table cheese. As it ages, the flavor is more pronounced. It is a super melting cheese and also good for grating when aged.

**Fior di latte** mozzarella is a creamy white *pasta filata* (stretched curd) cheese. It is made in Abruzzo, Molise, and Campania from either buffalo or cow's milk. It melts beautifully and has a delicate flavor.

**Fontina** is a delicate, nutty semihard cheese made in the Val d'Aosta region from cow's milk; it is creamy in texture when young and becomes drier with age. Do not confuse it with Danish fontina. Italian fontina is recognized by its brown rind.

**Gorgonzola** is a classic blue-veined cheese from the region of Lombardia with a buttery texture. Great as a melting cheese or in sauces.

**Grana padano,** a grainy, yellow, hard cow's milk cheese made throughout the Po Valley, is aged for eighteen months and has a grainy texture. It is an excellent table cheese when young and perfect for grating as it ages.

**Parmigiano-Reggiano,** the king of Italian cheeses, is a partially skimmed cow's milk cheese, aged for twenty-four months. Protected by law, it can only be made in certain provinces of Emilia-Romagna; it must be made from two successive milkings and must be aged at least twelve months. This is a fabulous table cheese, with a delicate nutty taste and a granular, crystallized texture. Recognize it by the pin dots on the rind spelling out the words *Parmigiano-Reggiano*. Aged, it is wonderful grated in pasta dishes.

**Pecorino,** made exclusively from sheep's milk in many regions of Italy, is a saltier but moist and crumbly hard cheese with a whiff of the barnyard. When aged, it is used primarily for grating. It can also contain black or green peppercorns. The word *pecorino* is embedded on the cheese rind.

**Provolone,** a cow's milk cheese originally made in Campania but now also made in Tuscany, is a firm and sweet-flavored cheese when young but gets more pronounced in flavor as it ages. It is cylinder shaped. This is an excellent grating cheese.

**Ricotta,** a fresh cheese made from the leftover whey of the cheese-making process either from cow's or sheep's milk, is made throughout Italy. It is used primarily as a filling. Salted and aged, it becomes ricotta salata.

**Scamorza,** shaped like a pear, is a combination cow's and sheep's milk cheese made in Campania, Molise, and Abruzzo. It is drier than other types of *pasta filata* cheese and can also be smoked.

It is recognized by its brownish yellow rind. Use it in cooking, cut into bits as a filling for vegetables, or mixed into casseroles.

**Taleggio** is a flat, rectangular cow's milk cheese from the Val Taleggio with a soft, creamy texture and an orange colored rind. It has a rich taste that gets more pronounced as it ages. Use it as a table cheese and in sauces.

Introduction

# HERBS AND SPICES

Herbs and spices can add just the right balance of flavor to casseroles. What is the difference between them? In simplest terms, spices are the fruits, berries, and roots of plants while herbs are the leaves of plants. Spices are usually purchased in either dried or powdered form, whereas herbs can be fresh or dried. Here are some pointers to keep in mind about buying, storing, and using them.

Fresh herbs versus dried herbs? No contest. Fresh are better because they release oil and that is where the flavor is. Rub a fresh rosemary leaf with your fingers and automatically its perfume is released; do that with dried rosemary and all you get is a medicinal smell because the oils have been lost to the drying process. Purchase fresh herbs that look healthy and do not look wilted or have dark spots. As soon as you get them home, wrap them in slightly damp paper towels and keep them in the vegetable bin of your refrigerator. Use them within a few days. Parsley, thyme, and marjoram will keep very well. Basil is more fickle and does not like cold or water on its leaves.

The best time to add fresh herbs to a dish is at the end of the cooking time if possible, so their flavor is not lost from a long cooking process.

Spices should be kept in a dark, cool place like a pantry; never store them next to the stovetop, as the heat from cooking can destroy their flavor. Do not buy spices in bulk jars unless you do massive cooking because their flavors wane after about six months. Buying small containers is best, especially for spices like cinnamon, cloves, and ginger.

# Catch of the Day
## *Casseroles*

Cacciucco alla Livornese
(Classic Fish Stew from Livorno)

Merluzzo Stufato
(Stewed Cod)

Tegamaccio
(Fish Stew Lago Trasimeno Style)

Casseruòla di Aragosta,
Gamberi e Finocchio
(Lobster and Shrimp Casserole
with Fennel)

Cassola
(Sardinian Fish Casserole)

Frutte di Mare in Padella
(Seafood Casserole)

Calamari Ripieni in Padella
(Stovetop Stuffed Squid Casserole)

Pesce al Marinaio
(Mariner's Casserole)

Pesci Misti con Biscotti
(Velvety Mixed Fish Casserole with
Buttery Cracker Topping)

Pomodori Ripieni con Tonno e
Patate
(Stuffed Tomatoes with Tuna and
Potatoes)

Tiella di Cozze
(Mussel Casserole)

Vongole e Pasta
(Clams and Pasta Casserole)

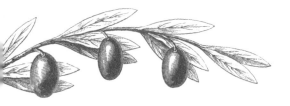

Fish and shellfish make terrific, quick casseroles but because they are delicate in texture, extra care needs to be taken when cooking with them. Fish and seafood casseroles require types of fish with firm flesh that will not disintegrate in cooking like swordfish, monkfish, sea bass, haddock, halibut, and salmon. Shellfish types good for casseroles include dry scallops, mussels, shrimp, clams, oysters, crab meat, and lobster.

Be aware of some simple rules when purchasing fish and seafood. Ask where the fish is from and if it has been frozen; many times fish is flash frozen as it is caught at sea and then delivered to market. Read the signs in the fish case that tell you if the fish is fresh or frozen and where it is from. If you live near the coast, try to buy the local catch if possible because that is a sure sign of freshness. Fish should always smell fresh with a hint of sweetness; smelly fish is not fresh. Be aware of how the fish looks; fish should look moist, not dry and yellow. Seafood like clams and mussels should not have cracked shells; scallops should look plump and milky. Shrimp come frozen in most cases but are defrosted for sale. It is best to buy them frozen and uncooked. Lobster can be cooked to order or ordered ahead of time. Refrigerate your purchase immediately and use the fish or seafood within a day.

Sauces for fish casseroles should not be too heavy because they can mask the flavor. A thin white sauce, or one made with fish stock, wine, or citrus are good choices.

# Cacciucco alla Livornese
## CLASSIC FISH STEW FROM LIVORNO

This dish originated with fishermen in Livorno who sold the best of their catch and used what was left over and unwanted at day's end to make a fish casserole or stew. A variety of fish went into the pot, including squid, monkfish, and cod. Tradition dictates that at least five different types of fish be used, one for each of the c's in the word *cacciucco*, which means mixture. This stew was traditionally cooked in an earthenware pot atop the stove. Begin by adding the fish that takes the longest time to cook. Make sure that all the fish is cut the same size for even cooking. From start to finish, this should take about 25 minutes. It is even better the next day. Crackling, crusty bread and a crisp salad make the meal both wholesome and complete.

MAKES ABOUT 2 QUARTS OR 8 SERVINGS

1 large onion, coarsely chopped
3 garlic cloves
¼ cup fresh Italian parsley leaves
8 fresh basil leaves
¼ cup olive oil
½ teaspoon hot red pepper flakes
⅔ cup dry white wine
2 cups fresh or canned peeled, diced plum tomatoes
1 cup clam juice, fish bouillon, or water
½ teaspoon fine sea salt or more to taste
½ pound cleaned squid, cut into 1-inch rings
½ pound swordfish, skinned and cut into 1-inch chunks
½ pound medium shrimp (about 13), shelled
¼ pound sea scallops
¼ pound monkfish, cut into 1-inch pieces
2 tablespoons fresh lemon juice
8 toasted bread slices

In a food processor or by hand mince the onion, garlic, parsley, and basil together. Heat the oil in a heavy pot and stir in the minced onion mixture. Cook over low heat until the ingredients soften, then stir in the pepper flakes and cook 1 minute longer.

Raise the heat to high, pour in the wine, and allow most of it to evaporate. Lower the heat and stir in the tomatoes, clam juice, and salt. When bubbles just begin to appear on the sides of the pot, begin adding the fish pieces in the order given, allowing the squid to cook for 5 minutes before adding the swordfish. Cook just until the fish turns opaque or whitish and flakes easily with a fork and the shrimp have turned pink. Stir in the lemon juice and correct the salt if necessary.

Ladle the soup over the bread slices and serve piping hot.

## Merluzzo Stufato
## STEWED COD

2 tablespoons olive oil

1 onion, diced

2 celery stalks, diced

2 cups coarsely chopped tomatoes, fresh or canned

1 tablespoon capers in brine, drained and minced

1 bay leaf

2 tablespoons chopped fresh Italian parsley leaves

2 pounds fresh cod, cut into 1-inch chunks

Fine sea salt to taste

It takes *molto pazienza* (a lot of patience) to prepare baccalà, a dried, salted cod that is as stiff as a board. Several slow soakings in water eventually transform it into plump white flesh that is the prime ingredient for *merluzzo stufato,* stewed cod. But here is a shortcut using fresh instead of dried cod to make the stew.

SERVES 4

Heat the olive oil in a large soup pot over medium heat. Stir in the onion and celery and cook until soft. Stir in the tomatoes, capers, bay leaf, and parsley and simmer covered for 3 to 4 minutes. Add the cod, cover, and simmer for about 8 minutes, until the fish easily flakes with a fork and looks opaque. Season with salt.

TIP: The stew can also do double duty as a sauce for spaghetti.

# *Tegamaccio*
## FISH STEW LAGO TRASIMENO STYLE

This delicate fish stew is typical of the cooking of the island of Isola Maggiore on Lago Trasimeno in Umbria. (The island is also known for its exquisite lace making.) Traditionally, a combination of eels, tench, perch, trout, whiting, and grayling goes into the stew, but use what is available, such as cusk, haddock, swordfish, and scallops. Make sure the fish are all cut the same size so everything cooks in about the same time.

SERVES 6

¼ cup olive oil plus more for drizzling
2 garlic cloves, minced
⅓ cup minced fresh Italian parsley leaves
½ teaspoon hot red pepper flakes
1 cup diced celery
6 cups diced fresh plum tomatoes
½ cup dry white wine
1 teaspoon salt
Freshly ground black pepper to taste
2 pounds assorted cleaned fish, cut into 1- or 2-inch chunks
6 toasted bread slices

Heat the olive oil in a sauté pan and when the oil begins to shimmer, add the garlic, parsley, pepper flakes, and celery; cook until the garlic and celery begin to soften. Stir in the tomatoes, wine, and salt and pepper. Lower the heat to simmer and add the fish. Cook slowly uncovered for 5 to 8 minutes, just until the fish easily flakes with a fork. Serve the fish in soup bowls over toasted bread slices. Pass olive oil to drizzle on top.

6 tablespoons unsalted
butter

½ cup pine nuts

1 pound medium shrimp,
in the shell

1 cup diced fennel (white
bulb only)

¼ cup unbleached all-
purpose flour

1 small, whole star anise,
ground to a powder

¾ cup cooking liquid from
shrimp

2 cups light cream

1 pound cooked lobster
meat, cut into bite-size
pieces

Salt to taste

2 tablespoons minced
fresh Italian parsley
leaves

# Casseruòla di Aragosta, Gamberi e Finocchio

## LOBSTER AND SHRIMP CASSEROLE WITH FENNEL

Italian lobster (aragosta) is smaller and sweeter than the species we get here. Since I live in New England, it seemed right to include a stovetop lobster and shrimp casserole with an Italian twist. With the addition of diced fennel and ground star anise, the flavor intensifies without being too overpowering in this delicate dish.

SERVES 4

Melt 1 tablespoon of the butter in a small sauté pan or skillet and toast the pine nuts until they are nicely browned. Transfer the nuts to a dish and set aside.

Put the shrimp in a medium pot, cover with 1½ cups cold water, add a pinch of salt, and bring to a boil. Lower the heat to medium and cook the shrimp just until the shells turn pink. This should take only a couple of minutes. Remove the pot from the heat and allow the shrimp to cool in the water. When cool, drain, reserving ¾ cup of the water. Peel the shrimp, discard the shells, and set the shrimp aside.

Melt the remaining butter in a 10×2-inch stovetop casserole dish. Stir in the fennel and cook it over medium heat just until it softens.

Whisk in the flour and the star anise until the mixture forms a paste-like consistency. Slowly whisk in the reserved cooking water and the cream. Continue whisking until the mixture looks smooth.

Gently fold in the lobster and shrimp until well blended. Season with salt. Stir in the parsley. Sprinkle the top with the nuts and serve.

> ✺ TIP: Lobster bodies and shrimp shells make an excellent stock when combined with aromatic vegetables such as carrots, celery, and onions. To make a simple shrimp stock, place the shells from 1 pound uncooked medium-size shrimp in a one quart saucepan and add 2½ cups water. Add 4 sprigs of Italian parsley tied in a bunch, 1 teaspoon sea salt, 1 stalk celery cut in half, and 1 small carrot. Bring to a simmer, cover, and cook for 30 minutes. Strain through a colander set over a bowl, press on the solids, and discard the solids. Stir in the juice of one lemon.

CIAO ITALIA SLOW AND EASY

# *Cassola*

## SARDINIAN FISH CASSEROLE

Sardinia has an important fishing industry and out of it comes some fabulous fish casseroles like *cassola*, which can also be considered a stew. To make sure all the fish is cooked at the same time, be sure to cut into uniform pieces.

SERVES 6 TO 8

Heat half the oil in an ovenproof sauté pan. Stir in the onion, garlic, and red pepper and cook slowly over medium heat until the vegetables soften. Stir in the tomatoes, wine, and salt and pepper. Bring the mixture slowly to a boil and cook for 2 to 3 minutes. Reduce the heat to low and cook, covered, for 10 minutes.

Meanwhile, sauté the squid in the remaining oil for 3 or 4 minutes. Slowly pour in the tomato mixture. Cover and simmer for 15 minutes. Add the remaining fish and cover and simmer for 15 minutes or until all the fish is fork tender. Serve in bowls over slices of toasted bread.

¼ cup olive oil
1 onion, coarsely chopped
2 garlic cloves, minced
1 small red chili pepper, chopped
2 cups chopped cherry tomatoes
¼ cup dry white wine
Salt and pepper to taste
2½ pounds mixed fish, such as squid rings, octopus, sole, halibut, and red mullet, cleaned and cut into 1-inch pieces
Toasted bread slices

## Frutte di Mare in Padella
### SEAFOOD CASSEROLE

2 tablespoons olive oil

2 medium leeks (white part only), diced

1 cup diced fennel (white bulb only)

1 medium red bell pepper, diced

¼ cup minced fresh Italian parsley leaves

Salt to taste

½ pound squid rings, fresh or frozen

1 pound swordfish, cut into 1-inch chunks

1 pound sea scallops, cut in half crosswise

1 pound medium shrimp, peeled

Juice of 2 limes

1 cup canned cannellini beans, drained and rinsed well

1 cup dry white wine

2 cups rinsed fresh spinach leaves, torn into pieces

This casserole is a takeoff on the traditional dish known as *frutte di mare* (fruits of the sea), which combines a variety of fish and shellfish in a vinaigrette.

SERVES 4 TO 6

Heat the olive oil in a cast iron or other skillet over medium-high heat. Stir in the leeks, fennel, bell pepper, and parsley and cook until the leeks begin to soften. Season the mixture with salt. Transfer the mixture to a dish.

Add the squid and swordfish to the pan and sauté until the squid and swordfish turn opaque. Stir in the scallops and the shrimp. Continue to cook for 3 to 4 minutes. Stir in the lime juice and season the mixture with salt. Return the diced vegetable mixture to the pan; stir the ingredients gently but well. Stir in the beans.

Raise the heat to high and pour in the wine and allow it to cook for 1 minute over high heat. Lower the heat, cover the pan, and simmer for 5 minutes. Uncover and scatter the spinach over the top of the fish. Cover the pan and cook for 2 or 3 minutes or just until the spinach has wilted.

Mix the spinach carefully into the ingredients and serve hot in soup bowls.

# Calamari Ripieni in Padella
## STOVETOP STUFFED SQUID CASSEROLE

Fresh squid are a delicacy in my book and perfect in this stovetop casserole. There are two types of squid: calamari and totani. The calamari is more tender than the totani. My general rule when cooking squid is to use very small ones for grilling and in seafood salads. Use larger ones for stuffing. Slow cooking ensures tenderness every time.

SERVES 4

½ cup olive oil
1 large garlic clove, minced
1 medium onion, minced
¼ pound bay scallops
1 teaspoon fine sea salt
1 teaspoon capers in brine, drained
½ cup fresh bread crumbs
4 fresh or frozen cleaned squid, about 6 inches long
2 large plum tomatoes, peeled, seeded, and diced
½ cup dry white wine
Freshly ground black pepper to taste

In a large skillet, heat ¼ cup of the olive oil. Add the garlic and onion and sauté the mixture for about 4 minutes. Add the scallops and continue sautéing quickly for 3 minutes.

Transfer the mixture to a bowl; add the salt, capers, and bread crumbs and mix well. Divide the mixture and stuff loosely into each squid body. Do not overpack the squid or they will split during cooking. Close the openings with toothpicks and set aside.

Heat the remaining ¼ cup olive oil in a large skillet, add the stuffed squid, and brown slowly over low heat for 5 minutes. Raise the heat to medium, add the tomatoes and wine, and cook for 2 minutes. Cover the skillet, lower the heat, and simmer for 15 to 20 minutes, until the squid are easily pierced with a knife. Serve immediately with some of the pan juices poured over the top.

2 cups crushed fresh or
canned tomatoes
1 tablespoon flour
1½ cups diced onions
2 tablespoons unsalted
butter
2 teaspoons salt
½ teaspoon white pepper
¾ teaspoon dried oregano
¼ teaspoon dried mustard
¼ teaspoon whole allspice
1-inch-long piece fresh
ginger, peeled
2 pounds haddock or
perch fillets, cut into
bite-size pieces
2 large eggs, slightly
beaten
2 tablespoons minced
fresh Italian parsley
leaves
2 tablespoons fresh lime or
lemon juice

# Pesce al Marinaio
## MARINER'S CASSEROLE

This hearty mariner's casserole made with haddock or perch fillets comes from the fishermen's wives of Gloucester, Massachusetts, a largely Sicilian community whose heritage has been tied to the sea for centuries. Serve this as a "stew" with crackers or rolls, or ladle it over cooked rice. The ginger and allspice provide an interesting flavor component.

SERVES 8

Put the tomatoes in a 2-quart stovetop casserole or Dutch oven. Stir in the flour and mix until smooth. Stir in the onions, butter, salt, pepper, oregano, and mustard.

Place the allspice and ginger in a small piece of cheesecloth; tie with kitchen twine and add to the pot. Cook the ingredients, covered, over medium heat for 15 minutes. Add the fish and cook for 10 minutes or until it easily flakes with a fork.

Remove the casserole from the stovetop and discard the cheesecloth bag. Whisk in the eggs and parsley, then the lime juice. Return the casserole to the stovetop and cook just until the mixture thickens slightly.

Serve hot.

# Pesci Misti con Biscotti

## VELVETY MIXED FISH CASSEROLE WITH BUTTERY CRACKER TOPPING

Mixed chowder fish is used to make this stovetop casserole with a cracker topping. Be sure all the fish pieces are cut the same size (about 2 inches) to ensure even cooking.

SERVES 4

Melt the butter for the cracker topping in a 9×2-inch stovetop casserole dish or cast iron skillet. Stir in the cracker crumbs and coat them well. Transfer them to a small bowl and set aside.

Toss the fish pieces, lemon juice, onion, and spinach together in a large bowl. Set aside.

To make the sauce, dissolve the bouillon cube in the water and set aside.

Melt the butter over medium heat in the same casserole dish used to brown the bread crumbs; whisk in the flour and continue whisking until a smooth paste is formed. Slowly pour in the bouillon and continue to whisk until the mixture begins to thicken; keep the consistency loose, not too thick. Season with salt. Stir in the tarragon and thyme. Lower the heat.

Transfer the fish mixture to the casserole dish, add the sauce, and gently combine.

Cover and cook the casserole over medium heat for 6 to 8 minutes, just until the fish easily flakes with a fork. Remove the cover. Sprinkle the crumbs over the top of the casserole and serve hot.

> TIP: Substitute frozen or fresh peas for the spinach.

### CRACKER TOPPING
5 tablespoons melted butter
1½ cups Ritz crackers, crushed

### FISH
2 pounds mixed cut-up chowder fish, such as haddock, cod, halibut, and monkfish
2 tablespoons fresh lemon juice
1 small onion, finely minced
1 pound spinach, stemmed, washed, drained, and torn into bite-size pieces

### SAUCE
1 fish bouillon cube
1¼ cups boiling water
2 tablespoons butter
2 tablespoons unbleached all-purpose flour
Salt to taste
2 tablespoons minced fresh tarragon
2 tablespoons minced fresh thyme

- 4 medium beefsteak tomatoes, stemmed and cut in half horizontally
- 4 small cooked red-skin potatoes, peeled and diced
- One 6-ounce can chunk tuna in olive oil
- 1 small red onion, cut into quarters
- 2 tablespoons capers in salt, rinsed well
- ¼ cup fresh Italian parsley leaves
- Extra virgin olive oil
- Salt to taste
- Coarsely ground black pepper to taste
- ¼ cup fresh bread crumbs

# Pomodori Ripieni con Tonno e Patate
## STUFFED TOMATOES WITH TUNA AND POTATOES

Beefsteak tomatoes make great containers for this tuna and potato casserole. The dish can stand alone as an easy and light lunch or supper, or serve it as a side to meat, fish, or poultry. Buy good quality Italian tuna in olive oil.

SERVES 4

Preheat the oven to 350°F.

Gently squeeze out and discard the seeds from the tomato halves. Spoon some of the pulp into a bowl and add the potatoes.

Flake the tuna with a fork in a separate bowl and then add it with its oil to the tomato and potato mixture.

Mince the onion, capers, and parsley together and add to the tomato mixture. Add salt and pepper to taste.

Divide and fill the tomato halves with the tomato mixture. Do not overpack them because they could split while baking.

Lightly oil a baking dish and sprinkle the bread crumbs in the dish. Place the tomatoes over the bread crumbs. Drizzle the tops with oil and bake for 30 minutes or until the tomatoes appear soft but not collapsed. These can be served hot or at room temperature.

# Tiella di Cozze
## MUSSEL CASSEROLE

One of the classic dishes of the region of Puglia (Italy's heel) is *tiella*, a mussel and potato casserole made in an earthenware pan. This dish is built of many layers and is said to be descended from the Spanish paella. There are countless versions of the dish, but all must contain potatoes. Be attentive when buying mussels and make sure that no shells are broken.

SERVES 4 TO 6

Preheat the oven to 375°F.

Scrub and rinse the mussels well. Pull away the beards and discard them. Throw away any mussels with cracked shells. Put the mussels in a sauté pan, add the wine, cover the pot, and steam them until the shells begin to open. Drain them in a cheesecloth-lined strainer or colander over a bowl. Reserve the liquid.

Remove the top shell of each mussel. Set the mussels aside. Spread the olive oil in a casserole dish. Arrange a layer of onions over the olive oil. Add a layer of tomatoes and a layer of potatoes. Place the mussels in their shells over the potatoes in a single layer.

Salt and pepper the mussels to taste.

Combine the cheese, bread crumbs, and parsley together in a small bowl. Sprinkle some of the mixture over the mussels. Continue making layers of onion, tomatoes, potatoes, mussels, and cheese.

Pour the reserved mussel liquid along the side of the pan. Pour the beaten egg over the top of the casserole.

Bake uncovered until the potatoes are browned, about 45 minutes. Use a spoon to scoop and serve.

3 pounds fresh mussels
½ cup dry white wine
¼ cup extra virgin olive oil
1 onion, thinly sliced
2 cups halved cherry tomatoes
1 pound all-purpose potatoes, such as russet, peeled and thinly sliced into rounds
Salt to taste
Coarsely ground black pepper to taste
¾ cup grated pecorino cheese
⅔ cup fresh bread crumbs
¼ cup chopped fresh Italian parsley leaves
1 large egg, slightly beaten

## Vongole e Pasta
### CLAMS AND PASTA CASSEROLE

3 tablespoons olive oil

2 large garlic cloves, slivered

10 ounces minced fresh clams, drained, liquid reserved

Fine sea salt to taste

¼ teaspoon freshly ground black pepper

¼ cup minced fresh Italian parsley leaves

2 tablespoons minced fresh basil

12 ounces rigatoni, cooked

4 anchovy fillets in oil, drained and cut into bits

1½ cups fresh or canned peeled, diced plum tomatoes (3 or 4)

8 oil-cured black olives, pitted and diced

1 teaspoon dried oregano

Clams and pasta are paired perfectly in this easy-to-do-ahead casserole. Cooking clams over low heat prevents them from becoming tough, so don't be in a hurry with them.

SERVES 4 TO 6

Preheat the oven to 325°F.

Brush a 13½×9-inch ovenproof casserole with 1 teaspoon of the olive oil. Set aside.

Heat 2 tablespoons of the olive oil in a sauté pan and slowly cook the garlic over medium heat until it just starts to turn golden brown. Remove and discard the garlic. Add the clams together with their juice. Cook for 2 minutes over medium-low heat. Stir in the salt, pepper, parsley, and basil and cook slowly until the liquid is reduced by half.

Combine the cooked rigatoni with the clam mixture, then transfer it to the casserole. Sprinkle the anchovies over the top, then the tomatoes, olives, and oregano. Drizzle the remaining 2 teaspoons of olive oil over the top. Bake uncovered for 15 to 20 minutes, until heated through. Serve hot.

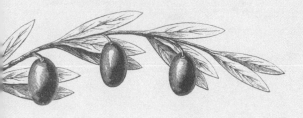

# Meat
## Casseroles

Bomba di Riso alla Mara
(Mara's Rice Bomb)

Braciola con Olive e Formaggio
(Stuffed Flank Steak with Olives and Cheese)

Polenta

La Bistecca di Fianco Imbottita
(Stuffed Flank Steak)

Involtini di Carne con Prosciutto
(Meat Rolls Stuffed with Ham and Herbs)

Brasato All'Aceto del Vino
(Braised Beef Roast in Wine Vinegar)

Casseruòla d'Agnello all'Erbe
(Lamb Stew with Herbs)

Coniglio Contadino al Vino Bianco
(Country-Style Rabbit with White Wine)

Costine con Rigatoni
(Sunday Night Beef Short Ribs with Rigatoni)

Lenticchie e Porri con Salsicce
(Lentils and Leeks with Sausage)

Spalla di Vitello con Spinaci e Carote
(Veal Shoulder, Spinach, and Carrot Casserole)

Ossobuco Tre Visi
(Veal Shanks with Tomatoes and Porcini Mushrooms)

Peposo
(Tuscan Tilemakers' Stew)

Polenta Pasticciata
(Layered Cornmeal Pie with Mushrooms and Sausage)

Prosciutto Cotto con Broccolo e Besciamella
(Ham and Broccoli Casserole in White Sauce)

Salsicce con Patate e Zucchine
(Pork Sausage with Potatoes and Zucchini)

Spezzatelle
(Lamb and Dandelion Casserole)

Spezzatino di Montone
(Lamb and Potato Casserole)

Stinco di Agnello con Orecchiette
(Lamb Shanks with Little Ear Pasta)

Stracotto alla Lombarda
(Lombardy-Style Stewed Beef)

LESS TENDER CUTS OF MEAT LIKE BEEF AND LAMB shoulder chops, pot roasts, chuck roast, veal shanks, veal breast, and short ribs are good choices for casseroles, especially braised casseroles, because during cooking the connective tissues of the meat break down, creating juiciness, tenderness, and lots of flavor. Leaner cuts like flank steak and round steak do not have as much connective tissue and tend to be drier; they are best cooked with liquids, herbs, and spices, which will result in a texture that is tender and juicy.

Most of the recipes in this chapter instruct you to brown the meat first to seal in juices. Do not rush this step; it is important to make sure that the meat is uniformly browned before adding other ingredients. Meat based casseroles always seem to taste better the next day, so there is an advantage to making them ahead. If you do, make sure to refrigerate the dish immediately after cooking to avoid the possibility of bacteria; never leave a meat casserole to cool first before refrigerating it. I use silicone hot pads to line the refrigerator shelf before placing a hot casserole on it; this will ensure that the heat from the dish will not crack the shelf. Several pot holders or towels will work, too. Another advantage to making casseroles ahead is that after cooling overnight, any fat will have risen to the top and solidified and can then be lifted off easily with a spoon before reheating.

Remember that cooked meat dishes should only be reheated once, otherwise they become a risk for food poisoning. And be sure to reheat meat until it is piping hot.

## PRAISING BRAISING

Braised meats, so popular in the fifties, have made a welcome comeback, because they are easy to prepare, perfect for fall and winter cooking, provide loads of saturated flavor, and are great do-ahead dishes that taste even better the day after they are made.

Braising is often the answer when it comes to cooking a less tender cut of meat like pork shoulder roasts, beef pot roasts, and veal breast roasts. Braising means that the meat is first allowed to brown in some type of fat. Olive oil and bits of pancetta (Italian bacon) give added flavor. The browning process is very important and should not be rushed so that all the surfaces of the meat are sealed and the sugars in the meat have begun to caramelize, producing a rich brown color. This will help to develop a delicious sauce as the meat is cooking. After browning, small amounts of liquid are added to prevent scorching, keep the meat moist, and create flavorful juices that can be spooned over the meat just before serving. Liquids can include broths or wine, pureed tomatoes or tomato sauce, or even beer. I am partial to using wine and find braising a good way to use up open bottles. Wine imparts a very nice depth of flavor and gives a rich color to the meat and juices. The seasonings are important, too. Make a bouquet garni, a small bundle of herbs such as sprigs of parsley, thyme, and rosemary tied together, and add some spices, such as whole peppercorns and cloves. Wrap these in cheesecloth and add to the dish as it cooks. Vegetables such as carrots, parsnips, chunks of onion, and fennel can be added and give marvelous flavor to braised dishes. My preference is to cook the dish covered in a low-temperature oven around 275°F to 300°F until the meat is fork tender. But stovetop cooking is fine, too, if the heat is kept at a simmer. And the best part is that once you have the dish in the oven or simmering on the stovetop, you can pretty much forget it.

When the meat is cooked, remove it from the pot to a cutting board. Carve the meat against the grain into thin slices and serve with some of the pan juices. When you make the meat ahead and refrigerate it, carve it while it is still cold before returning it to the pot and then reheat slowly.

An added bonus to braising is that leftovers make great sandwich fixings, or can be used in stir-fry or combined with pasta or rice.

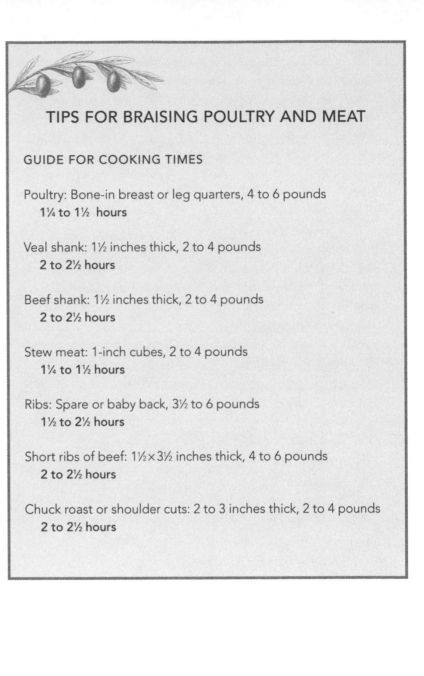

# TIPS FOR BRAISING POULTRY AND MEAT

## GUIDE FOR COOKING TIMES

Poultry: Bone-in breast or leg quarters, 4 to 6 pounds
   **1¼ to 1½ hours**

Veal shank: 1½ inches thick, 2 to 4 pounds
   **2 to 2½ hours**

Beef shank: 1½ inches thick, 2 to 4 pounds
   **2 to 2½ hours**

Stew meat: 1-inch cubes, 2 to 4 pounds
   **1¼ to 1½ hours**

Ribs: Spare or baby back, 3½ to 6 pounds
   **1½ to 2½ hours**

Short ribs of beef: 1½ × 3½ inches thick, 4 to 6 pounds
   **2 to 2½ hours**

Chuck roast or shoulder cuts: 2 to 3 inches thick, 2 to 4 pounds
   **2 to 2½ hours**

# Bomba di Riso alla Mara

## MARA'S RICE BOMB

*Bomba di riso* is an impressive molded rice dish that is a staple in the kitchen of my friend Mara Neviani, who lives in Cavriago. The origins of this dish are said to come from the town of Piacenza, where it is still prepared for the feast of the Assumption on August 15, known as Ferragosto. The procedure calls for the use of arborio rice, that short-grain starchy rice used to make risotto. The rice is boiled in either chicken or beef broth, then packed into a ring mold that is lined with overlapping slices of cooked ham. The center of the mold is filled with a meat ragù. The contrasting tastes of delicately flavored rice and intensely flavored ragù is a delight. This dish makes a great company presentation. The ragù can be made days ahead and the rice mold assembled a day prior to baking.

SERVES 8 TO 10

2 tablespoons butter
1 pound boiled ham, thinly cut into approximately 4½×6-inch-long slices
1 ounce dried porcini mushrooms
1 carrot
1 celery stalk, chopped
1 small onion, chopped
1 tablespoon extra virgin olive oil
1 garlic clove, minced
1 pound ground beef
1 pound canned, peeled plum tomatoes
1 tablespoon tomato paste
2 tablespoons minced fresh Italian parsley
Salt to taste
Coarsely ground black pepper to taste
6 cups chicken or beef broth
2½ cups arborio rice
5 tablespoons grated Parmigiano-Reggiano cheese
¼ cup heavy cream

Lightly butter a 9×2¼-inch ring mold with some of the butter. Line the mold with the ham slices, overlapping them slightly so no gaps appear and allowing a 2-inch overhang on the rim of the mold. Cover the mold loosely with plastic wrap and refrigerate until ready to fill.

Place the mushrooms in a bowl, cover with warm water, and let soak for 30 minutes. Drain the mushrooms, reserving the liquid, then dice and set aside.

Mince the carrot, celery, and onion together with a chef's knife.

Heat the olive oil and 1 tablespoon of the butter in a saucepan, stir in the carrot, celery, and onion, and cook the vegetables over low heat until they are soft. Stir in the garlic and cook it until it begins to soften. Stir in the ground beef and cook it until it loses its pink color.

In a bowl mix together the tomatoes, tomato paste, and ½ cup of the reserved porcini liquid and add it to the beef mixture. (Save the remaining porcini liquid to use when making soups or stocks.) Stir in the parsley, salt, and pepper. Cover the pan and simmer the ragù for 1½ hours. Ten minutes before the ragù is cooked, stir in the mushrooms.

The consistency of the mixture should be very thick with almost no liquid. Keep the ragù warm while the rice is cooking.

Bring the broth to a boil in a soup pot. Stir in the rice, cover, and cook, stirring occasionally until all the broth is absorbed. Stir in the cheese, the remaining butter, and the cream.

Preheat the oven to 350°F.

Pack the rice evenly into the mold and fold over the ham hanging around the edges to cover the rice as much as possible. Place the mold in a baking pan large enough to hold it and carefully pour hot water into the baking pan, allowing it to come up to about 1 inch along the sides of the ring mold. Bake for 25 minutes or until the rice is hot. Remove the mold from the water bath and run a butter knife around the inside edge of the mold to loosen the ham and ensure that it will unmold. Place a serving dish larger than the mold over the top and invert the mold onto the dish. Fill the center of the mold with some of the ragù. Put the remaining ragù in a bowl to pass separately. To serve, cut the mold into wedges and spoon some of the ragù on the side.

TIP: A water bath, called a *bagno maria,* is used when heat must be evenly and slowly distributed during cooking.

# Braciola con Olive e Formaggio
## STUFFED FLANK STEAK WITH OLIVES AND CHEESE

Flank steak is a flat, boneless cut of meat found on the underside of the cow right below the loin and sirloin sections. This well-used muscle is fibrous and less tender than other cuts. To bring out flavor and to tenderize, it is usually marinated and grilled. But it can also be elevated to a party dish when butterflied (sliced open horizontally down the longest side but not all the way through so that it lies flat like an open book) and stuffed with cheese, pancetta, and olives. Bake it in a slow oven, and what emerges is a very tender piece of meat with a saucy sauce that is just right for serving over polenta.

SERVES 4 TO 6

Preheat the oven to 325°F.

Brown the pancetta in the olive oil in a 10½×2½-inch ovenproof sauté pan. Transfer the pancetta with a slotted spoon to a medium bowl and set aside.

Mince together the garlic, parsley, and olives and transfer to the bowl with the pancetta.

Butterfly the meat with a sharp chef's knife: Hold the knife parallel to the longest side of the meat. Begin slicing through the meat, cutting all the way through the center to the other end, but not through the end. The meat should remain in one piece. Flatten the two ends out so they look like an opened book.

Rub the meat with the salt and pepper. Spread the pancetta mixture evenly over the meat. Sprinkle the minced eggs over the pancetta mixture.

Sprinkle the cheese evenly over the eggs.

Start at the longest side of the meat and roll it up tightly like a jelly roll and tie it in several places with kitchen string.

Brown the meat on all sides in the pancetta drippings; if the pan is dry, add a little olive oil.

¼ pound pancetta, diced
1 teaspoon olive oil
3 whole garlic cloves, peeled
¼ cup minced fresh Italian parsley leaves
12 oil-cured black olives, pitted
1½ to 2 pounds flank steak
1½ teaspoons coarse salt
¼ teaspoon coarsely ground black pepper
2 hard-boiled eggs, minced
¼ pound Asiago cheese, grated
Kitchen string
1½ cups whole baby carrots
1½ cups sliced fennel (white bulb only)
One 28-ounce can crushed tomatoes
1 cup dry red wine
Polenta for serving (see page 27)

Add the carrots and fennel to the pan.

Combine the tomatoes and wine in a bowl. When the meat is well browned, turn off the heat and pour the tomato mixture evenly over the meat.

Cover the pan tightly and bake until the meat is fork tender, 1 to 1½ hours.

Transfer the flank steak to a cutting board; remove and discard the strings. Let the flank steak rest for 5 to 10 minutes to allow for better cutting into even slices. If cooking ahead of time, refrigerate the meat for several hours, or overnight, and then cut into 1-inch rounds.

Return the meat to the pan and reheat slowly in the sauce. Serve as is or with polenta.

> ✂ TIP: Flank steak needs to be cut across the grain to break the meat fibers; otherwise it will be too tough.

# Polenta

I like a loose-consistency polenta for this dish, so I do not cook it long; for a firm consistency, cook for 12 to 15 minutes.

Whisk the cornmeal in the water and milk.

Using a whisk, stir and cook the mixture in a heavy pot over medium heat; when the polenta begins to thicken and pull away from the sides, it is done. Season with salt, pepper, and grated pecorino cheese.

Spread a scoop of polenta in the middle of a dinner plate and place a slice or two of the flank steak over the polenta, and spoon some of the vegetables and sauce on top.

1 cup stone-ground
   cornmeal
2 cups water
1 cup milk
Freshly ground black
   pepper to taste
Pecorino cheese, grated,
   to taste

## La Bistecca di Fianco Imbottita
### STUFFED FLANK STEAK

1 pound flank steak, cut into two 8-ounce strips and butterflied as for recipe on page 25

Salt to taste

Grinding black pepper

8 cured olives, pitted

1 large garlic clove, peeled

1 small red onion, peeled and cut into quarters

½ cup packed well-squeezed cooked spinach

½ cup grated Parmigiano-Reggiano cheese

¼ cup red wine

¾ cup prepared tomato sauce

2 tablespoons olive oil

Here is another version of stuffed flank steak. Cutting the meat into two pieces and then butterflying them as for the recipe on page 25 saves baking time.

SERVES 4

Preheat the oven to 325°F.

Flatten out the meat pieces and rub them with salt and pepper. Mince the olives, onion, and garlic together in a food processor or by hand. Transfer the mixture to a bowl and add the spinach. Mix well and season with salt and pepper to taste.

Divide and spread the mixture over the meat pieces, spreading it evenly and thinly. Divide and sprinkle the cheese over the pieces.

Mix the tomato sauce and red wine together in a small bowl and set aside.

Roll each piece of meat up like a jellyroll and tie with kitchen string in the middle and at both ends; be careful that the filling does not fall out.

Heat the olive oil in an oven-to-table casserole dish just large enough to hold the meat. Brown the pieces well on both sides.

Turn off the heat and pour the sauce evenly over the meat. Cover with a lid or heavy-duty aluminum foil and bake until fork tender, about 45 minutes to 1 hour.

Allow the meat to stand covered for 10 minutes. Remove the string and discard. Allow the meat to rest covered for 5 minutes before cutting it into ½-inch thick slices. Serve with some of the sauce spooned over them.

# Involtini di Carne con Prosciutto

## MEAT ROLLS STUFFED WITH HAM AND HERBS

Thin slices of veal or chicken cutlet or boneless pork chops can be made into *involtini,* stuffed, rolled bundles with a savory filling. This dish has a nice woodsy flavor provided by fresh sage and juniper berries. Use a good red wine such as the 2001 Cabernet Sauvignon from Bighorn Cellars to make the sauce. This is a great company dish.

SERVES 4

8 thin slices veal, pork, or chicken

8 thin slices prosciutto di Parma

2 tablespoons finely crushed juniper berries

8 fresh sage leaves

Freshly ground black pepper to taste

Fine sea salt to taste

Extra virgin olive oil

½ cup Cabernet Sauvignon, such as 2001 Bighorn Cellars

Lay the meat pieces flat. Top each one with a slice of prosciutto, a little of the crushed juniper berries, a sage leaf, a grinding of pepper, and sprinkling of salt. Roll each piece up to form a little bundle. This is the involtino. Tie the involtini with kitchen string. Put them in a buttered baking dish.

Preheat the oven to 350°F.

Brush the involtini with olive oil. Bake them for 5 minutes, then pour in the wine and continue baking for an additional 7 minutes. Baste the bundles occasionally with the wine and bake them for about 12 minutes. Serve hot.

> TIP: Juniper berries are in the spice section of most grocery stores; use a mortar and a pestle to crush them or use a small spice grinder.

# Brasato all'Aceto del Vino

## BRAISED BEEF ROAST IN WINE VINEGAR

2 pounds chuck or top
round roast
3 garlic cloves, slivered
Salt and freshly ground
black pepper to taste
1 tablespoon olive oil
1 large onion, diced
⅔ cup red wine vinegar
1 pound whole baby
carrots
2 cups cauliflower florets,
cut into 1-inch pieces
1 tablespoon tomato paste
¼ cup minced fresh Italian
parsley
¼ cup minced fresh basil

Red wine vinegar is the secret ingredient for the zing in this braised chuck roast with baby carrots and cauliflower. Using a heavy Dutch oven keeps even heat, and the small amount of liquid keeps the ingredients moist. This dish can be cooked stovetop or in the oven.

SERVES 4 TO 6

Dry the roast well with paper towels. Make slits all over the roast with a small knife and insert the garlic slivers. Rub the roast with salt and pepper.

Heat the olive oil in a Dutch oven over medium-high heat. Brown the roast on all sides, then lower the heat. Add the onion and cook for 5 minutes or until it begins to wilt. Add ⅓ cup of the vinegar, carrots, and cauliflower and cook for 5 minutes.

Mix the tomato paste and the remaining ⅓ cup wine vinegar together in a small bowl and add it to the roast. Cover the pot and simmer the roast for about 1 hour and 45 minutes or until a knife is easily inserted into the meat. (For oven braising, cook the roast in a Dutch oven in a preheated 275°F oven for 2 hours or until fork tender.) Add the parsley and basil to the pot about 5 minutes before the meat is done.

Transfer the meat to a cutting board and let it rest for 10 minutes. Then cut it into slices and return it to the pot with the vegetables. Reheat slowly. Serve the meat directly from the Dutch oven with some of the vegetables and pan juices.

VARIATION: Add fennel strips, red bell pepper strips, and sliced mushrooms for variety.

# Casseruòla d'Agnello all'Erbe
## LAMB STEW WITH HERBS

From the region of Basilicata in southern Italy comes this simple lamb casserole; the flavor is enhanced by the combination of herbs. For added flavor, add a small hot red pepper.

SERVES 6 TO 8

Preheat the oven to 325°F.

Dry the meat pieces well with paper towels.

Heat 2 tablespoons of the olive oil over medium-high heat in a stovetop-to-oven casserole dish or sauté pan. Brown the meat pieces on all sides, salt and pepper them, and transfer to a bowl.

Add the remaining oil to the pan and cook the onion until it softens; add the potatoes and garlic and cook for 2 minutes.

Return the meat pieces and any juices to the pan, placing the pieces on top of the potatoes.

Combine the tomatoes in a bowl with the herbs. Pour the mixture over the meat and potatoes.

Bake for 1½ to 2 hours or until the meat is fork tender. Uncover and sprinkle with the cheese. Bake uncovered for an additional 5 minutes.

> ✀ TIP: If using canned whole plum tomatoes, use scissors to cut the tomatoes into pieces in the can.

2 pounds lamb stew meat, cut into 1-inch chunks
¼ cup olive oil
Salt and freshly ground black pepper to taste
1 onion, finely chopped
1 pound red-skin potatoes, cut into chunks
1 garlic clove, minced
8 fresh or canned plum tomatoes, finely chopped
2 tablespoons chopped fresh mint
1 tablespoon minced fresh rosemary
1 teaspoon dried oregano
½ cup grated pecorino cheese

2 pounds rabbit, cut into
    serving pieces
Juice of 2 large lemons
½ cup unbleached all-
    purpose flour
1 teaspoon salt
½ teaspoon coarsely
    ground black pepper
3 tablespoons olive oil
⅓ pound pancetta or salt
    pork, diced
1½ cups chopped onion
1 tablespoon fresh
    rosemary leaves
1 cup dry white wine,
    preferably Soave or
    Pinot Grigio
1 cup fresh or frozen peas

# Coniglio Contadino al Vino Bianco
## COUNTRY-STYLE RABBIT WITH WHITE WINE

Italians are quite fond of rabbit dishes. The delicate meat blends well with many seasonings and sauces. The demand for rabbit is not as high at home as in Italy, but if you make this recipe, you will be surprised at the delicacy and flavor. Soaking the rabbit in water and lemon juice helps to eliminate any gamy taste.

SERVES 6

Place the rabbit pieces in a bowl and add cold water to cover. Add the lemon juice and refrigerate, covered, overnight.

Preheat the oven to 350°F.

Remove the pieces from the water and dry them well with paper towels. Combine the flour, salt, and pepper in a large paper bag. Place the pieces in the bag, close the bag, and shake well to coat all the pieces. Shake off the excess flour. Set the pieces aside.

In a large ovenproof skillet or casserole dish, heat the olive oil over medium-high heat. Add the rabbit pieces and brown them on all sides. Transfer them to a dish. Add the pancetta or salt pork and cook for 2 minutes. Stir in the onion and cook until they soften. Return the rabbit pieces to the dish and sprinkle the rosemary over them. Lower the heat to a simmer.

Pour in the wine and add the peas and salt and pepper to taste. Cover the dish with foil and bake for 35 minutes or until the pieces are tender.

Serve from the baking dish and spoon the vegetables and pan juices over the pieces.

# Costine con Rigatoni

## SUNDAY NIGHT BEEF SHORT RIBS WITH RIGATONI

I cook this beef short rib and rigatoni casserole for Italian friends who don't often have this cut of meat. It is the perfect winter dish for a Sunday night supper. Short ribs are meaty and high in connective tissue and come from the chest area. The success of this dish really depends on meaty, not fatty ribs, so get to know your butcher and look for well marbled ribs without excess fat. Ask for an English cut, which means pieces that are between 2 and 4 inches long. Slow cooking produces the most tender and most delicious flavor, and the entire casserole can be assembled and cooked hours before it is needed and just reheated, or cooked the day before. Either way, it is a winner.

SERVES 4

1 tablespoon olive oil
8 meaty short ribs on the bone (about 4 pounds), 1½ inches thick and 4 inches long
Salt and freshly ground black pepper
¼ pound pancetta, diced
1 medium onion, diced
1 cup diced fennel (white bulb only)
2 carrots, diced
3 garlic cloves, minced
8 to 10 shiitake mushrooms, stems removed, caps cut in half
⅔ cup red wine
1 teaspoon hot red pepper flakes
1 teaspoon dried oregano
One 28-ounce can crushed plum tomatoes
2 tablespoons balsamic vinegar
1 pound rigatoni or other short cut of pasta, such as penne or bow ties
Grated Parmigiano-Reggiano cheese for sprinkling

Preheat the oven to 300°F.

Heat the olive oil in a large (12 × 2½-inch) stovetop-to-oven casserole. Rub the ribs with salt and pepper and brown them in batches. Do not crowd the ribs or they will steam instead of brown. As they brown transfer them to a dish.

If there is a lot of fat in the pan, drain off most of it, leaving about 2 tablespoons, and brown the pancetta; stir in the onion, fennel, and carrots and cook over medium heat, stirring occasionally until the vegetables begin to soften. Stir in the garlic and cook for 2 minutes. Stir in the mushrooms and cook for 2 minutes more. Raise the heat to high and pour in ⅓ cup of the wine. Cook until the wine almost evaporates, about 3 minutes.

Stir in the red pepper flakes and oregano.

Combine the remaining wine, tomatoes, and balsamic vinegar in a bowl; mix well, then pour over the ribs.

Cover the pan tightly with a sheet of heavy-duty aluminum foil and then with a lid and bake for 2 hours or until the ribs are tender. Correct the seasoning.

Remove the ribs to a cutting board; trim the meat away from the bone and connective tissue, cut into small pieces and return the meat to the pan. Discard the bones and connective tissue. Keep the ragù warm while the rigatoni cooks.

Bring 4 quarts of water to a rolling boil; add 1 tablespoon of salt and the rigatoni; cook until al dente. (no white flour is visible when a piece is broken in half).

Drain the rigatoni and return it to the pot. Ladle some of the ragù over the rigatoni and mix well. Transfer the rigatoni to a platter and pour the ragù over pasta. Or, mix the rigatoni directly in the casserole dish and serve.

Sprinkle the top with grated Parmigiano-Reggiano cheese.

CIAO ITALIA SLOW AND EASY

# *Lenticchie e Porri con Salsicce*
## LENTILS AND LEEKS WITH SAUSAGE

Lentils are synonymous with the cooking of the landlocked region of Umbria, and the most famous are the creamy lentils of Castelluccio, grown on the plains near the Sibillini mountains. This tender pulse retains its shape in cooking and requires no presoaking. Lentils lend a nutty flavor to this leek and sausage casserole, as well as providing loads of protein.

SERVES 4 TO 6

1 tablespoon olive oil
1½ pounds sweet Italian sausage links
¼ cup diced pancetta
1 large leek (white bulb only), cut into thin rings
2 celery stalks, diced
1 large carrot, peeled and diced
2 garlic cloves, minced
½ cup dry red wine
2 cups coarsely chopped plum tomatoes
Salt and freshly ground black pepper to taste
1½ cups lentils
5 cups low-sodium vegetable or beef stock

Preheat the oven to 325°F.

Pour the olive oil into a Dutch oven or similar heavy oven-to-table pot and brown the sausage along with the pancetta over medium-high heat. Transfer the sausage and pancetta to a dish and set aside.

Sauté the leek, celery, and carrot in the pan drippings until they soften. Stir in the garlic and cook until it softens.

Raise the heat to high and pour in the wine; allow it to come to a boil. Lower the heat to a simmer and stir in the tomatoes. Season with salt and pepper. Stir in the lentils.

Return the sausage and pancetta to the pan and cover the mixture with the vegetable or beef stock.

Cover the pan and bake for 35 to 40 minutes, until most of the liquid has evaporated.

## Spalla di Vitello con Spinaci e Carote
## VEAL SHOULDER, SPINACH, AND CARROT CASSEROLE

⅓ cup olive oil

2 pounds bone-in veal shoulder chops

Salt and freshly ground black pepper to taste

1 large onion, finely minced

3 garlic cloves, finely minced

1 small dried hot red pepper, crushed, or 1 teaspoon hot red pepper flakes

4 cups prepared tomato sauce (page 99)

1 cup cooked carrots or peas

1 pound fresh spinach, stemmed, washed, and drained

6 or 7 fresh basil leaves torn into pieces

½ pound *paccheri*, or large rigatoni, cooked and kept warm

Grated pecorino cheese for sprinkling

This tasty casserole evolved from some leftover cooked carrots, a bag of forgotten spinach in the far recesses of the refrigerator, half a bag of *paccheri* (a large rigatoni-shaped pasta without lines), leftover tomato sauce, and some veal shoulder chops that I had just purchased. I got to work and made this dish, which surprised and evoked great satisfaction from my husband, who deemed it lip-smacking good . . . especially when accompanied by a glass of Silverado Sangiovese 1977.

SERVES 4

Preheat the oven to 325°F.

Heat the olive oil in a large (12 × 2½-inch) stovetop-to-oven casserole dish over medium-high heat. Season the veal chops with salt and pepper and brown them quickly on both sides. Transfer them to a dish. Stir in the onion and cook until it begins to soften. Stir in the garlic and hot pepper. Cook until the garlic softens. Return the chops to the pan with any juices that have collected.

Cover the chops with the tomato sauce. Cover the casserole with a lid or aluminum foil and place in the oven.

Bake for 45 minutes to an hour, until the meat is fork tender. Remove the casserole from the oven. Transfer the chops to a cutting board and trim the meat away from the bones. Discard the bones and return the meat to the pan.

Put the carrots and spinach on top of the meat. Return the casserole, covered, to the oven and cook for 2 or 3 minutes longer, until the spinach has wilted.

Remove the casserole from the oven. Stir in the basil and the cooked pasta and serve immediately. Pass the cheese.

> TIP: Use a Microplane grater to finely mince unpeeled garlic cloves; it works well on fresh ginger as well.

# Ossobuco Tre Visi

## VEAL SHANKS WITH TOMATOES AND PORCINI MUSHROOMS

They are proud of their cuisine at Ristorante Tre Visi, where the food reflects the cooking of the city of Vicenza and the Veneto region. I had a wonderful lunch there sampling air-dried cod (*stoccafisso*) cooked in the Vicentine style with onions, anchovy, and cheese, as well as *baccalà mantecato*, dried cod in the Venetian style, made by pounding the cod in a mortar and pestle while adding extra-virgin olive oil drop by drop. The second course was ossobuco, veal shank, long simmered in tomato sauce with porcini mushrooms. Ossobuco means a bone with a hole in it, and the marrow in the center of the bone is considered a delicacy. This is a great company dish because it can be made several days ahead of time. Serve it on top of creamy polenta.

SERVES 4

¾ cup (about 1 ounce) dried porcini mushrooms
1 tablespoon extra virgin olive oil
¼ pound pancetta, diced
1 carrot, scraped and diced
1 onion, diced
1 celery stalk, diced
⅓ cup minced fresh Italian parsley leaves
1 large garlic clove, thinly sliced
2½ pounds veal shanks
One 28-ounce can whole plum tomatoes
¾ cup dry red wine
3 to 4 fresh thyme sprigs
Freshly ground black pepper to taste
1½ teaspoons fine sea salt
Polenta for serving (see page 27)

Preheat the oven to 300°F.

Place the porcini mushrooms in a bowl, pour ¾ cup hot water over them, and set aside.

Heat the olive oil in a heavy ovenproof 12×3-inch sauté pan. Stir in the pancetta, carrot, onion, celery, parsley, and garlic and cook over medium heat, stirring occasionally, until the vegetables begin to soften.

Push the mixture to one side of the pan and add the veal shanks. Brown the shanks on both sides, then redistribute the vegetable mixture around them.

In a bowl mix the tomatoes and wine together. Pour the liquids slowly over the veal shanks. Add the thyme, pepper, and salt. Cover the pan and bake the shanks for 1½ to 2 hours.

Halfway into the cooking stir in the porcini mushrooms and their liquid. Cover the pan and continue cooking until the meat is fork tender. Serve the ossobuco over polenta.

1 large carrot, peeled and
 cut into quarters
1 medium onion,
 quartered
1 celery stalk, cut in half
3 large sprigs fresh Italian
 parsley
4 whole garlic cloves,
 peeled
4 whole fresh basil leaves
2 tablespoons fresh thyme
2 tablespoons fresh
 marjoram
1 tablespoon fresh mint
2 tablespoons fresh
 rosemary leaves
4 whole fresh sage leaves
⅓ cup extra virgin olive oil
1¾ pounds stew beef,
 trimmed of all visible fat
 and cut into 1-inch
 cubes
1½ teaspoons fine sea salt
1 tablespoon coarsely
 ground black pepper
1 bay leaf
1 cup vin santo or moscato
 (Muscat) wine
2 cups hot beef broth
1 tablespoon whole green
 peppercorns in vinegar,
 drained
Zest of 1 lemon
3 ripe William, Anjou, or
 Bartlett pears

# *Peposo*
## TUSCAN TILEMAKERS' STEW

Beef stew with pears? This antique Tuscan casserole is called *peposo* (from the word *pepe* for "pepper"), and its origins go back to tilemakers who prepared a *calderone* (big pot) of stew and placed it at the mouth of the *fornace* (oven) while they made clay tiles. The stew was left to cook for many hours, which resulted in deliciously tender meat in a beautiful sauce made with *vin santo* (holy wine). In today's Tuscan kitchen, pears have been replaced by tomatoes and this old-fashioned dish is more commonly referred to as *peposo dell'Impruneta*, taking its name from the town of Impruneta near Florence, where the tiles that are famous all over the world (*cotto dell'Impruneta*) are still made. Vin santo is made in many areas of Italy and is a beautiful amber-colored, high-alcohol dessert wine. If it is not available, use a good moscato (Muscat) wine.

For quick work in the kitchen, use a food processor to mince the vegetables and herbs. Make the dish several days ahead and refrigerate to really meld the flavors.

SERVES 4 TO 6

In a food processor or with a chef's knife, mince together the carrot, onion, celery, parsley, garlic, basil, thyme, marjoram, mint, rosemary, and sage. Set the mixture aside.

In an ovenproof 10½ × 2½-inch pan, heat 2 tablespoons of the olive oil. Stir in the minced vegetables and herbs and sauté them, stirring occasionally, until they soften, but do not let them brown. Transfer the ingredients to a dish and set it aside.

Preheat the oven to 275°F.

Dry the meat with paper towels and sprinkle with salt and pepper. Add the remaining olive oil to the pan and when the oil begins to shimmer, add the bay leaf and meat and sauté, turning it to brown. When there is no more liquid in the pan, raise the heat to high, add the wine, and allow it to reduce by half. Lower the heat and pour in enough of the beef broth to cover the meat. Return the vegetable mixture to the pan and stir in the peppercorns and the lemon zest. Cover the pan and bake for 1 hour.

Peel and core the pears. Dice two of the pears, then cover and set aside. Puree the remaining pear in a food processor or blender until it is smooth. Cover and set aside.

Stir the pureed pear into the meat mixture. Cover the pan and bake for an additional 1½ hours, adding more broth if necessary. Five minutes before the meat is done, remove the bay leaf and add the diced pears.

Serve the stew in soup bowls accompanied with crusty bread.

This stew can be made ahead and refrigerated for several days.

## Polenta Pasticciata

### LAYERED CORNMEAL PIE WITH MUSHROOMS AND SAUSAGE

- ⅔ cup dried porcini mushrooms
- 3 cups water
- 3 cups milk
- 2 to 2¼ cups stone-ground cornmeal
- 6 tablespoons unsalted butter, cut into bits
- 1½ pounds sweet Italian pork sausage, removed from the casing
- 2-2½ cups prepared tomato sauce (page 99)
- Salt and freshly ground black pepper to taste
- 1 cup grated Parmigiano-Reggiano cheese

Some of the finest cornmeal comes from the region of Lombardia and is the basis for many classic dishes including this *polenta pasticciata*, a layered cornmeal pie. It is best to use stone ground cornmeal because some of the nutritious hull and germ are maintained, but if it is not available, regular cornmeal will do. It won't have the same texture, however.

SERVES 6 TO 8

Put the mushrooms in a bowl and cover with hot water. Set aside and allow them to rehydrate for at least 30 minutes. This step can be done a day ahead.

Combine the water and milk in a large saucepan; stir in the cornmeal and whisk it until it's blended with the liquid. Cook the cornmeal over medium-high heat, whisking constantly until the polenta thickens and begins to leave the sides of the pan and forms a loose ball.

Scoop the polenta out onto a lightly oiled large cutting board or baking sheet and spread it evenly into a 17 × 12 rectangle. Allow it to cool. It is best to refrigerate the polenta for an hour before cutting it or make it ahead and hold it covered overnight in the refrigerator.

Melt 1 tablespoon of the butter in a sauté pan and cook the sausage until it is browned. Drain the mushrooms, reserving the water. Chop the mushrooms and add them to the pan with the sausage. Stir in the tomato sauce and cook for 20 minutes. Add ¼ cup of the porcini liquid and cook for 20 minutes longer. Season with salt and pepper.

Butter a 9 × 12-inch casserole dish.

Spread a thin layer of the sausage sauce in the base of the dish.

Cut the polenta in half crosswise to fit the dish and place one half of the polenta in the dish over the sauce. Spread half of the remaining sauce and half of the butter over the polenta and sprinkle with some of the cheese.

Make a second layer of polenta and top with the rest of the sauce. Sprinkle the remaining cheese and butter.

Bake uncovered until the cheese is nicely browned and the casserole is hot. Let the casserole stand for about 5 minutes before cutting.

# Prosciutto Cotto con Broccolo e Besciamella

## HAM AND BROCCOLI CASSEROLE IN WHITE SAUCE

A spectacular baked ham is often the main feature on holiday tables, but what do you do with leftovers when you are weary of ham and cheese sandwiches? You make this delicious and easy-to-put-together casserole with broccoli, onions, and cheese all nestled nicely under a thin blanket of white sauce made with low-fat milk. The dish can either be baked in the oven or cooked stovetop and can also be assembled a day ahead of time. And the best thing is that the recipe is so generic that substitutions are endless, such as leftover spinach, or baked squash, or carrots, or peas in place of the broccoli.

SERVES 4 TO 6

1 tablespoon olive oil
1 medium onion, coarsely chopped
¾ pound broccoli, stemmed and cut into ½-inch florets
2 tablespoons butter
2 tablespoons unbleached all-purpose flour
2 cups warm lowfat milk
Salt and freshly ground black pepper to taste
3 cups cubed ham
1 cup grated Parmigiano-Reggiano cheese

Heat the olive oil in the casserole (use an 11½×2-inch enameled cast iron oven-to-table or similar pan) over medium heat and stir in the onion and broccoli. Cook, stirring occasionally, until the broccoli stems begin to soften. Partially cover the pan while it is cooking.

Transfer the broccoli and onions to a dish. Set aside.

Preheat the oven to 350°F.

Melt the butter in the casserole and whisk in the flour until a smooth paste is obtained; slowly pour in the milk and cook over medium heat until the sauce begins to thicken. At this point salt and pepper the sauce.

Return the broccoli and onions to the casserole and mix in with the ham.

Sprinkle the top evenly with the cheese, cover, and bake for 30 to 35 minutes, or cook covered over medium-low heat on the stovetop until heated through.

> TIP: Scrape the broccoli stems with a vegetable peeler and use them in a stir-fry.

1 pound good quality
   Italian sweet or spicy
   sausage
1 medium onion, thinly
   sliced
1 large red-skin potato, cut
   into ¼-inch-thick slices
2 medium zucchini,
   trimmed and cut into ½-
   inch chunks
Salt and freshly ground
   black pepper to taste

# Salsicce con Patate e Zucchine
## PORK SAUSAGE WITH POTATOES AND ZUCCHINI

The success of this effortless-to-put-together casserole depends on the quality of the pork sausage; I usually make my own but when you are in a hurry, good store-bought sweet or spicy sausage will do. Everything goes into a heavy oven-to-table dish and cooks covered at a low temperature for 40 to 45 minutes, creating a delicious sauce. Vary the vegetables by using carrot chunks or brussels sprouts.

SERVES 3 TO 4

Preheat the oven to 325°F.

Put the sausage in a stovetop-to-oven baking dish at least 12 inches in diameter. Pour in ½ cup water and place over medium-high heat. Cover the pan and cook the sausage for 2 minutes on each side or until it just turns gray. Move the sausage to the center of the pan, scatter the onions around the outside of the pan, layer the potatoes over the onions, and the zucchini over the potatoes. Sprinkle everything with salt and pepper.

Bake covered for 40 to 45 minutes or until the sausage is cooked and the vegetables are tender. Serve with some of the pan juices.

# *Spezzatelle*
## LAMB AND DANDELION CASSEROLE

This casserole from the region of Puglia leads a double life. On the one hand, the combination of lamb stew meat and dandelion greens can be considered a casserole; on the other hand the airy and cheesy egg topping gives it a more debonair soufflé look. Whatever you choose to call it, it is delicious and easy to make. It is a good example of one of those classic regional dishes that are almost lost to time. Don't be put off by the onion and garlic powder; it is critical to the taste of the lamb. Trust me.

SERVES 4 TO 6

2½ pounds (a large bunch) dandelion greens, stemmed

3 tablespoons extra virgin olive oil

1 pound cubed lamb stew meat

1 teaspoon onion powder

½ teaspoon garlic powder

1 fresh or canned tomato, seeded and chopped

2 tablespoons minced fresh Italian parsley

1 tablespoon minced rosemary leaves

4 large eggs

½ cup crumbled goat cheese

1 cup grated Parmigiano-Reggiano cheese

½ cup diced mozzarella cheese

Fill a large pot with water and bring it to a boil.

Meanwhile clean the dandelions (which are notoriously sandy) by soaking them in several changes of cold water. Drain and add to the pot of boiling water. Cook uncovered for about 5 minutes; this will remove some of the bitterness. Drain in a colander, reserving 1 cup of the cooking water, squeeze out some of the water, and chop coarsely. Set aside. Keep the reserved water hot.

Heat the olive oil in a large, ovenproof 3½-quart casserole and brown the meat pieces. Sprinkle the meat with the onion and garlic powders. Stir in the tomato, parsley, and rosemary and cook for another 2 minutes. Stir in the dandelions and turn off the heat.

Preheat the oven to 400°F.

Whisk the eggs together in a large bowl, then whisk in the cheeses one at a time until the mixture is thick and well blended.

Pour the egg and cheese mixture evenly over the top of the meat and dandelion greens. Bake uncovered for 50 minutes or until the top is nicely browned and puffed.

Remove the spezzatelle from the oven; the topping will collapse somewhat. Cut into the casserole with a knife to make four to six wedges. Use a large spoon to lift the wedges out of the casserole and serve them in individual soup bowls. Pour some of the reserved dandelion water over the top of each wedge and serve immediately.

¼ cup olive oil

4 large baking potatoes, peeled and sliced ¼ inch thick

Salt to taste

Coarsely ground black pepper to taste

3 whole garlic cloves, peeled

½ cup fresh Italian parsley leaves

3 tablespoons rosemary leaves

2 pounds lamb stew meat, cut into 1-inch chunks

½ cup grated pecorino cheese

1 cup white wine or water

# Spezzatino di Montone
## LAMB AND POTATO CASSEROLE

Lamb and potatoes seasoned gently make a great one-dish dinner, add interest to a buffet table, and couldn't be easier to put together. It's sure to become a favorite of lamb lovers.

SERVES 6 TO 8

Preheat the oven to 350°F.

Pour half the olive oil into a 9×13-inch baking pan or 12×2½-inch round casserole dish and coat the pan on all sides with the oil to make serving easier.

Layer half the potatoes in the bottom of the pan. If some slices are thicker than others, use these on the bottom layer. Sprinkle salt and pepper over the layer of potatoes. Mince the garlic, parsley, and rosemary together and sprinkle half of it over the potatoes in the pan. Arrange the lamb pieces evenly over the layer of potato slices.

Add more salt and pepper and drizzle the rest of the olive oil over the lamb. Sprinkle the cheese over the lamb. Layer the rest of the potatoes over the top. Sprinkle salt and pepper and the rest of the herb mix over the potatoes.

Pour ½ cup of the wine or water along one side of the pan.

Bake uncovered for 1 hour. Add ½ cup more wine or water to the pan and bake for another hour or until a fork easily pierces the meat and the potatoes are browned.

> ✤ TIP: Do not buy cooking wines. They are full of added sulfites and salt. Wines that you enjoy drinking are also good for cooking.

# Stinco di Agnello con Orecchiette
## LAMB SHANKS WITH LITTLE EAR PASTA

Lamb shanks are a great cut of meat for braising or slow cooking; they tend to have little fat and lots of connective tissue. Braising allows that tissue to break down and produces rich, succulent, and very tender meat that is falling off the bone. In this preparation, the meat is removed from the bone, cut into bite-size pieces, and served with orecchiette, a dried pasta from Puglia readily available in your grocery store. To save time, bake the shanks one day, refrigerate, and save for combining with the orecchiette. Save the unused tomato sauce and freeze for another meal. This recipe is courtesy of my good friend and cooking teacher Anna Nurse.

SERVES 4

½ cup olive oil
4 meaty lamb shanks (3½ to 4 pounds)
4 garlic cloves, cut in half
1 large onion, chopped
Dried hot red pepper flakes to taste
¾ cup dry red wine
¾ cup tomato paste
6 cups prepared tomato sauce (page 99)
5 large fresh basil leaves
Salt to taste
1 pound orecchiette
Grated pecorino cheese for sprinkling

Preheat the oven to 325°F.

Heat the olive oil in an oven-to-table casserole dish or baking pan large enough to hold the lamb shanks. When the oil is hot, add the shanks and brown them evenly on all sides, a few at a time. Transfer the lamb shanks to a dish. Discard all but ⅓ cup of the oil remaining in the pan.

Add the garlic to the pan and cook over medium-low heat until the garlic is golden brown. With a slotted spoon, remove the garlic and discard it. Add the onion to the pan and cook over medium-low heat until soft, about 15 minutes. Add the pepper flakes. Increase the heat to medium-high, pour in the wine, and allow most of it to evaporate, about 3 minutes. Stir in the tomato paste with a wooden spoon and scrape up any bits of meat that are stuck to the bottom of the pan.

Return the lamb shanks to the pan and cover them with the tomato sauce. Cover the dish and bake for 2½ hours or until the meat is fork tender.

Remove the shanks to a cutting board and cut the meat away from the bones into bite-size pieces. Add the meat to the sauce. Stir in the basil and salt to taste. Keep the sauce warm and covered.

When ready to serve, cook the orecchiette in 4 to 6 quarts of rapidly boiling water to which 1 tablespoon of salt has been added. Orecchiette take a little longer to cook than other types of dried pasta because of their concave shape. They are cooked when there is no trace of white flour remaining when bitten into; the orecchiette should retain their shape and be al dente, firm but cooked.

Drain the orecchiette, reserving 2 tablespoons of the cooking water. Transfer the orecchiette to a serving dish. Mix 2 cups of the tomato sauce with the reserved water and pour over the orecchiette. Mix well. Serve immediately with a sprinkling of cheese.

# Straccotto alla Lombarda
## LOMBARDY-STYLE STEWED BEEF

The success of this classic stewed beef from Lombardy in the north of Italy depends on several things: the marinating time (overnight is best), the use of a good red wine, like Barolo, and the flavoring of the onions with pancetta, Italian bacon. Once cooked, it is even better the next day, served atop slices of golden polenta. The word *stracotta* means to cook a long time, and about 2 hours will do it for this recipe.

SERVES 6

3 pounds boneless rump or eye round roast

2½ cups dry red wine such as Barolo

1 cup diced onion

1 large garlic clove, minced

1 celery stalk, diced

¼ teaspoon freshly ground nutmeg

2 bay leaves

2 whole cloves

4 tablespoons (½ stick) butter

½ cup diced pancetta

2 tablespoons unbleached all-purpose flour

Salt and freshly ground black pepper to taste

Place the meat in a Dutch oven or similar deep casserole just large enough to hold it. Add the wine, half the onion, and the garlic, celery, nutmeg, bay leaves, and cloves. Cover the meat and refrigerate for several hours or overnight, turning the meat occasionally.

When ready to cook, drain the meat from the marinade and wipe it dry with paper towels. Drain the vegetables and reserve. Save the marinade.

Wipe the Dutch oven or casserole dry, and melt the butter. Add the pancetta and the remaining onion. Sauté for 3 or 4 minutes, until the pancetta just begins to crisp and the onion is soft. Transfer the mixture to a plate and reserve.

Coat the meat with the flour, shaking off the excess, and add it to the drippings in the pan. Brown the meat well on all sides. Return the pancetta mixture to the pan along with the reserved vegetables. Cook slowly for 5 to 10 minutes. Add salt and pepper and pour in the reserved marinade. Bring the mixture to a boil, then lower the heat to a simmer, cover the pot, and cook for about 2 hours or until the meat is tender.

Transfer the meat to a platter. Remove the bay leaves and cloves and discard them. Place the remaining liquid and vegetables in a food processor or blender and pulse until smooth. Slice the meat and top with the sauce.

> ✄ TIP: The meat will slice better if you allow it to stand tented with a sheet of aluminum foil for 15 minutes.

# Pasta
## Casseroles

Conchiglioni Ripieni al Forno
(Large Shells Stuffed with Ragù and
Cream)

Fusilli ai Tre Formaggi
(Fusilli with Three Cheeses)

Lasagne ai Carciofi e Ricotta
(Lasagne with Artichokes and Ricotta
Cheese)

Lasagne in Padella ai Carciofi e
Formaggio
(Skillet Lasagne with Artichokes and
Cheese)

Millerighi con Prosciutto di Parma
(Pasta Tubes with Savory Prosciutto
Filling)

Penne Integrale al Ragù
(Whole Wheat Penne with Meat Sauce)

Pappardelle con la Salsa di
Agnello e Vino di Sciampagna
(Lamb Stew in Champagne Sauce with
Pappardelle)

Rigatoni con Broccoli Rabe
(Rigatoni with Broccoli Rabe)

Timballo di Maccarun
(Molded Macaroni Casserole)

Timballo di Melanzane e
Bucatini
(Eggplant and Bucatini Casserole)

Timballo di Mezzi Ziti
(Baked Macaroni Casserole Pugliesi
Style)

Timballo di Pane e Formaggio
(Bread and Cheese Casserole)

Timballo di Scamorza
(Scamorza Cheese Casserole)

Timballo alla Teramano
(Crepes with Spinach and Veal,
Teramano Style)

Pasticcio di Maccheroni
(Sicilian-Style Chicken Pie)

SOPHIA LOREN, ON BEING ASKED HOW SHE MAIN-tained such a gorgeous physique, replied: "Everything you see I owe to pasta." Well said, because a diet without pasta is unthinkable to Italians.

Pasta in some form has been around for centuries. Water and flour mixed together makes a dough, a paste, from which the word is derived. The Egyptians made it, as well as the Greeks, the Romans, and the world at large. Though we will never know just who invented pasta, what we do know is that the Italians perfected it and made it their national dish. So much so that today it is considered one of the most important comfort foods and the basis for many casseroles. Pasta casseroles define weekend suppers in my house and are a perfect buffet addition.

There are over 350 types of pasta, many with endearing names like farfalle (butterflies), fusilli (twisted pasta), orecchiette (little ears), and linguine (little tongues). Short cuts or long cuts, they are all ideal for casseroles because they combine well with a myriad of other ingredients and sauces.

In this chapter you will find classic and contemporary casseroles—casseroles with whole wheat pasta, impressive molded pasta casseroles, and a new take on stovetop lasagne. Enjoy them all in moderation, and you will know exactly why Sophia Loren was right.

## THE ROLE OF PASTA IN CASSEROLES

Can any type of pasta be used in a casserole? Well, yes and no.

It all depends on what the other ingredients in the dish are and how they will be put together. For casseroles with slices or chunks of vegetables and meat, it is best to choose thicker cuts of pasta like rigatoni, fusilli, and even elbow macaroni because they complement the texture of the other ingredients. For molded types of casseroles like the eggplant timballo (page 66) and the *timballo di maccarun* (page 64), a thicker cut of pasta or a short cut of pasta is also best because the dish will be unmolded and thicker cuts will give structure and solidity, whereas using a thinner type like cappellini (angel hair) could result in a collapsed dish. For cheese-based casseroles, short cuts of pasta like penne with lines, fusilli, shells, and bow ties are best because their shapes trap sauce. For filled pasta such as the millerighi (page 59), it is important to use a brand that will hold up twice in the preparation, once when the pasta is partially cooked and drained, then when filled and baked. Always be sure that the pasta you are buying is made from 100 percent semolina flour. Semolina is the hardest of wheat flour and the key ingredient in Italy for making pasta secca, or dried pasta. Those made with enriched flour are starchier and gummy in texture. There are many good Italian brands of pasta on the market including Delverde, DeCecco, Barilla, Rienzi, and La Molisana.

# Conchiglioni Ripieni al Forno
## LARGE SHELLS STUFFED WITH RAGÙ AND CREAM

The original recipe for these large stuffed pasta shells (conchiglioni) comes from the kitchen of Signora Alba d'Aurora in Rome. I was a little skeptical when I scanned the ingredients—so much heavy cream and butter. I substituted low-fat milk for the besciamella (white sauce) and cut down on the cream, and the result was great taste with no guilt. Make the ragù a day or two ahead. The entire dish can be assembled a day ahead and refrigerated, leaving just the final steps of adding the cream and milk before baking. In the original recipe, the shells are filled uncooked and then baked, but if you wish, parboil them first, then fill them; this will cut down on the baking time. One or two of these rich ragù-stuffed shells are very filling, and I recommend serving them as part of a buffet.

MAKES 36 TO 40 (SERVES 20 FOR A BUFFET,
8 TO 10 AS A PASTA COURSE)

### RAGÙ
1 tablespoon extra virgin olive oil
¾ pound ground pork
½ cup dry red wine
1 cup prepared tomato sauce (page 99)

### WHITE SAUCE
4½ cups low-fat milk
8 tablespoons (1 stick) butter
½ cup unbleached all-purpose flour
½ teaspoon fine sea salt

One 12-ounce package large (2-inch) pasta shells
½ cup milk
1½ cups heavy cream
½ cup grated Parmigiano-Reggiano cheese

In a large skillet, heat the olive oil over medium heat. Add the meat and cook, stirring, until browned. Raise the heat to high, stir in the wine, and let most of it evaporate. Lower the heat to medium, add the tomato sauce, and cook, uncovered, for 15 minutes, or until thickened. Set aside.

Scald the milk (bring to just under a boil) in a saucepan. Set aside.

In another large saucepan, melt the butter. Whisk in the flour to make a smooth paste, and cook, stirring, for about 1 minute. Slowly whisk in the hot milk, and cook, whisking, until the sauce thickens enough to coat the back of a spoon. Stir in the salt. Remove from the heat, and stir in the ragù until well blended. Transfer the ragù to a bowl, cover, and refrigerate it for several hours or make it a couple of days ahead. This will make it easier to fill the shells.

Preheat the oven to 375°F.

To parboil the shells, bring 4 quarts of water to a boil; stir in 1 tablespoon of salt and the shells. Boil for 3 to 4 minutes; drain the shells in a colander and allow them to cool until easy to handle. Alternatively, do not parboil. Proceed to fill them as directed in the following step but decrease the baking time by 10 minutes.

Lightly butter a 14×8-inch baking dish. Using a spoon, fill the shells with the ragù mixture and place them close together in the baking dish.

Combine the milk and heavy cream in a bowl. Slowly pour evenly over the shells. Sprinkle the cheese over the top. Cover with aluminum foil and bake for 45 minutes. Serve immediately.

> ✄ TIP: Keep a ready supply of prepared tomato sauce in your freezer.

# *Fusilli ai Tre Formaggi*
## FUSILLI WITH THREE CHEESES

We all have our signature casseroles and this fusilli with three cheeses and spinach is one that my husband, Guy, craves. I often vary the ingredients, sometimes leaving out the spinach, and adding mushrooms or peas—no matter how I make it, he always claims it is his favorite comfort casserole. This is the perfect choice for a country buffet or potluck supper

SERVES 6 TO 8

½ pound ground pork
½ pound ground chuck
1 tablespoon olive oil
Salt and freshly ground
    black pepper to taste
4 cups prepared tomato
    sauce (page 99)
1 pound fusilli, bow ties, or
    elbow macaroni
½ cup cubed Italian fontina
    cheese
Two 8-ounce balls
    mozzarella cheese, cut
    in small pieces
½ cup grated Parmigiano-
    Reggiano cheese
2 cups shredded fresh
    spinach

Brown the ground pork and ground chuck in the olive oil in a Dutch oven or similar pot. Season with salt and pepper. Stir in 2 cups of the tomato sauce and simmer the mixture uncovered for 5 minutes.

Preheat the oven to 350°F.

Cook the fusilli until still quite firm (about 5 minutes) in 4 quarts rapidly boiling salted water. Drain and transfer the fusilli to the Dutch oven. Stir in the fontina, half of the mozzarella, and the Parmigiano-Reggiano cheeses over low heat. Off the heat stir in the spinach and the remaining tomato sauce.

Bake the casserole covered for 20 minutes, uncover, and scatter the remaining half of the mozzarella cheese over the top. Continue baking for 10 to 15 minutes, until the casserole is bubbly and the cheese has melted.

> TIP: Cheeses should always be well wrapped and stored in the warmest part of your refrigerator. Always bring them to room temperature before using.

2 tablespoons olive oil

2 garlic cloves, minced

One 9-ounce package frozen artichoke hearts, thawed and thinly sliced (or 4 fresh medium artichokes prepared according to the recipe on page 105)

1 pound whole milk ricotta cheese, drained, if watery, in a cheesecloth-lined strainer

½ cup grated Parmigiano-Reggiano cheese

2 tablespoons lemon zest

¼ cup minced fresh Italian parsley

2 large eggs

Salt and freshly ground black pepper to taste

4 cups prepared tomato sauce (page 99)

1 package no-boil lasagne sheets (preferably Delverde)

# Lasagne ai Carciofi e Ricotta
## LASAGNE WITH ARTICHOKES AND RICOTTA CHEESE

Probably the most popular casserole next to macaroni and cheese or chicken pot pie is lasagne packed with ricotta cheese, oozing with melted mozzarella cheese, and topped with tomato sauce. The next time you are in the mood for lasagne, try this version from Rome with artichoke hearts and ricotta cheese. To save time, frozen artichoke hearts are used in the recipe, but fresh artichokes can be substituted, cleaned as on page 105.

SERVES 8

Heat the olive oil in a sauté pan and cook the garlic until it softens. Add the artichoke slices and cook over medium heat, stirring occasionally, for 2 minutes. Set aside.

Combine the ricotta and Parmigiano-Reggiano cheeses in a bowl; stir in the lemon zest, parsley, eggs, and salt and pepper. Mix well. Stir in the artichoke pieces. Set aside.

Preheat the oven to 350°F.

Spread a thin layer of tomato sauce in the bottom of a 9×12-inch casserole dish. (If using Delverde lasagne sheets, use the pan that the noodles are packed in.) Place one layer of lasagne noodles over the sauce; if they do not fit perfectly, break them to fit or overlap them.

Spread a layer of the ricotta and artichoke mixture over the noodles and then a thin covering of tomato sauce. Continue making layers, ending with a top layer of noodles. Cover the top completely with sauce.

Cover the dish tightly with aluminum foil and place it on a baking sheet to absorb any drips.

Bake for 50 to 55 minutes, until the noodles are soft and the lasagne is very hot. Uncover and bake 5 minutes longer. Remove the casserole from the oven and allow it to sit for 5 minutes before cutting.

TIP: Whole milk ricotta works best in this recipe, yielding a creamy taste.

# Lasagne in Padella ai Carciofi e Formaggio
## SKILLET LASAGNE WITH ARTICHOKES AND CHEESE

In Italian, it's lasagne, not lasagna; the word is derived from the Roman *lasanum,* meaning a pot for cooking. In ancient Rome, the flat, wide noodles made with water and hard durum wheat (semolina) were air dried to preserve them. In old Italian cooking manuscripts, there are references to these wide noodles cooked in broth and sprinkled with cheese, not layered and stuffed, a far cry from what has come to be known in this country as lasagne. But things do change and here is a change from oven-baked lasagne to a nifty stovetop version, using no-boil noodles. A cast iron skillet or similar heavy pan like Le Creuset will work nicely. The beauty of this technique is that the lasagne is ready in about 25 minutes. Be aware that the quality of no-boil lasagne sheets can vary. Purchase a good brand like Delverde, which is used in this savory artichoke and cheese lasagne.

SERVES 4 TO 6

One 15-ounce container of fresh, skim, or whole milk pasteurized ricotta cheese, well drained

1 egg white

5 frozen cooked artichoke hearts from a 9-ounce package, defrosted and thinly sliced

2 tablespoons minced fresh Italian parsley

One 8-ounce ball mozzarella cheese, cut into bits

Salt and freshly ground black pepper to taste

3 cups prepared tomato sauce (page 99), plus extra to pass

4 no-boil 8×8-inch lasagne sheets (preferably Delverde)

½ cup grated Parmigiano-Reggiano cheese for sprinkling

Combine the ricotta cheese, egg white, artichoke slices, parsley, mozzarella cheese, and salt and pepper in a medium bowl. Set aside.

Spread 1 cup of the tomato sauce in the bottom of a 10×2-inch cast iron skillet or similar heavy sauté pan.

Place 1 lasagne sheet over the sauce; do not worry that the sheet does not fit exactly; it will expand while it cooks.

Spread one-third of the ricotta cheese mixture evenly over the lasagne sheet. Scatter about 2 tablespoons of the tomato sauce over the cheese.

Make two more layers like the first, ending the top layer with the last lasagne sheet. Spread 1¼ cups of the tomato sauce evenly over the top and sprinkle with the Parmigiano-Reggiano cheese.

Cover the skillet tightly with a sheet of heavy-duty aluminum foil and then a lid, slightly pressing it on the aluminum foil. Do not worry if the cover does not lie flat on top of the skillet; as the lasagne cooks, it will shrink.

Place the skillet over medium-low heat and cook the lasagne for 25 to 35 minutes or until noodles are soft. Make sure the heat is medium-low so the bottom will not burn. Uncover and check to see if the noodles are tender and cooked through. If not, re-cover the skillet and cook a bit longer.

Serve the lasagne directly from the skillet and pass extra tomato sauce if desired.

# Millerighi con Prosciutto di Parma

## PASTA TUBES WITH SAVORY PROSCIUTTO FILLING

*Millerighi* (meaning thousand lines because of the pasta's ridges), is a large tubular dried pasta that houses a savory stuffing. Similar to millerighi are the more familiar manicotti (meaning little muffs or sleeves) that are usually stuffed with ricotta cheese and served with tomato sauce. For a change, how about a savory prosciutto di Parma or ham stuffing baked under a blanket of creamy white sauce?

SERVES 6

Cook the pasta in 4 to 6 quarts of rapidly boiling water to which 1 tablespoon of salt has been added. Cook until al dente, about 4 minutes; the pasta should remain a bit firmer than normal because it will be baked in the oven and it is much easier to stuff when firm.

Drain them, cool, and set aside while making the sauce.

To make the sauce, melt the butter in a 2-quart saucepan over medium heat. When the butter begins to foam, whisk in the flour and make a smooth paste. Slowly add the milk and continue whisking until the sauce thickens enough to coat the back of a spoon. Stir in the fontina cheese, thyme, and salt. Keep the sauce warm and covered.

To make the filling, heat the olive oil in a sauté pan and stir in the onion; cook until the onion begins to wilt. Stir in the garlic and cook until the garlic softens. Stir in the prosciutto; cook for a couple of minutes. Stir in the carrots. Transfer the mixture to a bowl and stir in the cheese and ½ cup of the white sauce and salt to taste. Cool the mixture until easy to handle. Lightly butter two baking dishes.

Preheat the oven to 350°F.

Use a spoon or your hands to fill each pasta tube with some of the prosciutto mixture and place the tubes in a single layer in the baking dishes. Cover them with the remaining sauce and sprinkle the grated Parmigiano-Reggiano cheese evenly over the top.

Cover the dishes with aluminum foil and bake them for 30 to 35

12 large tubular pasta (either millerighi or manicotti)

**WHITE SAUCE**
6 tablespoons butter
6 tablespoons unbleached all-purpose flour
3 cups hot milk
2 cups fontina cheese, cut into bits
2 tablespoons fresh thyme leaves
Salt to taste

**FILLING**
¼ cup virgin or extra virgin olive oil
1 onion, minced
2 garlic cloves, minced
3 cups diced prosciutto di Parma or cooked ham
½ cup grated carrots
½ cup grated Parmigiano-Reggiano cheese

Salt to taste
⅓ cup grated Parmigiano-Reggiano cheese

minutes; uncover the dishes and bake 5 to 10 minutes longer, until the top is nicely browned. Serve two per person as a first course, or use as a main dish for a buffet.

> ✿ TIP: Soft cheeses like fontina will cut better if you use a tomato knife, sometimes called an angel food cake knife.

# Penne Integrale al Ragù
## WHOLE WHEAT PENNE WITH MEAT SAUCE

Whole wheat penne, slant-cut tubular pasta with lines, provides nutty flavor and guilt-free enjoyment in this homey ragù-style casserole. And even though the ingredients are humble, the addition of cream provides just enough richness to make this anything but ordinary tasting.

SERVES 6

2 tablespoons olive oil
1 small onion, minced
½ pound ground chuck
1 zucchini, grated
2 cups whole cherry
   tomatoes
Salt and freshly ground
   black pepper to taste
½ cup heavy cream
1 tablespoon dried
   oregano
½ cup minced fresh basil
½ pound whole wheat
   penne, cooked al dente
⅔ cup grated pecorino
   cheese

Preheat the oven to 350°F.

Heat the olive oil in a 10×2-inch casserole dish with a lid, such as Le Creuset or a similar ovenproof dish. Cook the onion over medium heat until it wilts; stir in the ground chuck and brown well. Stir in the zucchini and cook, stirring well, for 2 to 3 minutes. Add the cherry tomatoes and salt and pepper. Cook covered for 5 minutes over medium heat. Uncover the dish, lower the heat, and stir in the cream. Stir the oregano and basil into the mixture.

Stir in the penne and combine well with the sauce. Sprinkle the top with the cheese.

Cover the dish and bake for 35 to 40 minutes. Serve hot.

> TIP: An alternative to fresh cherry tomatoes is canned pomodorini (cherry tomatoes) such as Famoso, available in Italian grocery stores.

- 2 tablespoons olive oil
- 1 large garlic clove, minced
- 1½ pounds lamb stew meat, cut into bite-size pieces
- 1 cup champagne
- 1 cup hot beef broth
- 5 fresh or canned plum tomatoes, peeled, seeded, and chopped
- 1½ teaspoons fine sea salt
- ¼ teaspoon coarsely ground black pepper
- 2 tablespoons unbleached all-purpose flour
- ¼ cup half-and-half
- 8 fresh basil leaves, torn into pieces
- 1 pound pappardelle

# Pappardelle con la Salsa di Agnello e Vino di Sciampagna

## LAMB STEW IN CHAMPAGNE SAUCE WITH PAPPARDELLE

The story goes that this dish featuring pappardelle, wide noodles combined with lamb stew meat, comes from Caserta. It was made for a hungry traveling soldier by a beautiful peasant girl named Beatrice, who captured his love by adding champagne to the sauce.

SERVES 6

Heat the olive oil in a 14-inch sauté pan over medium heat. Stir in the garlic and cook until it softens. Raise the heat to high; add the lamb pieces and brown well. Reduce the heat to medium, pour in ½ cup of the champagne, stir for 4 minutes, and allow the foam to subside. Reduce the heat to a simmer and stir in the broth, tomatoes, and salt and pepper. Cover the pan and let simmer until the meat is tender, 45 to 55 minutes.

Drain the meat in a mesh strainer set over a bowl to catch the liquid. Set the meat aside in a separate bowl. Return all but ¼ cup of the liquid to the pan (there should be 2 cups of liquid) and stir in the remaining ½ cup of champagne. Cook uncovered over low heat until the mixture begins to simmer.

Whisk the flour into the reserved ¼ cup of liquid, then whisk it into the simmering sauce and cook until the mixture begins to thicken. Whisk in the half-and-half and continue to cook for 2 minutes.

Turn off the heat, return the lamb to the pan, and stir in the basil. Cover the sauce and keep warm while the pappardelle are cooking.

Cook the pappardelle in 4 to 6 quarts of rapidly boiling salted water until al dente. Drain them, reserving 2 tablespoons of the water, and return them to the pasta pot. Stir in the sauce and reserved cooking water. Mix well and transfer the mixture to a platter.

> TIP: For even browning of the meat pieces, dry them well on paper towels and do not crowd them in the pan, otherwise they will steam instead of brown.

# Rigatoni con Broccoli Rabe
## RIGATONI WITH BROCCOLI RABE

What could be better than a rigatoni casserole with sweet Italian sausage, broccoli rabe, and red bell peppers? This is the perfect tailgate casserole or Saturday night supper with a mixed green salad and poached pears for dessert.

SERVES 6 TO 8

1 pound broccoli rabe, ends trimmed

1 pound sweet Italian sausage links

1 tablespoon olive oil, plus more as needed

½ cup minced onion

4 garlic cloves, minced

1 large red bell pepper, seeded and diced

1 teaspoon hot red pepper flakes

Salt and freshly ground black pepper to taste

One 28-ounce can crushed plum tomatoes

1 pound cooked rigatoni

1 cup Asiago or Parmigiano-Reggiano cheese, grated

Cook the broccoli rabe in a large skillet with just the water clinging to its leaves until it is wilted. Drain in a colander, let cool, then cut coarsely and transfer to an oven casserole dish at least 12×2½ inches. Set aside.

Cook the sausage in the same skillet with ½ cup water until it turns gray; discard the water and brown the sausage links in its own fat; if the pan is dry, add a little olive oil. Transfer the sausage to a cutting board and cut into 1-inch pieces. Transfer the pieces to a bowl.

Put 1 tablespoon olive oil in the skillet and cook the onion, garlic, and diced bell pepper until the mixture begins to soften. Stir in the pepper flakes. Season the mixture with salt and pepper.

Mix the tomatoes with ½ cup water in a bowl and add to the skillet with the onion and pepper mixture. Add the sausage pieces to the skillet. Cover the pan and cook for 20 minutes over medium heat.

Preheat the oven to 350°F.

Combine the cooked rigatoni with the broccoli rabe in the casserole dish. Carefully pour the tomato and sausage mixture over the rigatoni and combine the ingredients well. Add salt and pepper.

Scatter the grated cheese over the top; cover and bake for 35 to 40 minutes, until heated through and piping hot.

# Timballo di Maccarun

## MOLDED MACARONI CASSEROLE

4 cups cooked elbow
macaroni (2 cups dried)

1½ cups diced mozzarella
cheese (fior di latte)

½ cup diced sharp
provolone cheese

2½ cups prepared tomato
sauce (page 99) plus
extra to pass

Olive oil for greasing

7 slices prosciutto di
Parma or ¼ pound
pancetta cut into thin
rounds

¾ pound ground chuck

½ pound ground pork

2 slices stale white bread,
crusts removed

2 large eggs, lightly
beaten

3 tablespoons minced
fresh basil

¼ cup minced fresh Italian
parsley

Salt and freshly ground
black pepper to taste

⅔ cup grated pecorino
cheese

1 teaspoon minced garlic

There are so many commonly prepared and predictable macaroni casseroles and then along comes this *timballo di maccarun*. *Timballo* is a word that means drum: in this case, a beautifully molded casserole made in a springform pan to give a drum effect. *Maccarun* is a southern dialect word for macaroni. The casserole is fun and easy to assemble, and makes an impressive statement. Put it together all at once or in stages.

SERVES 8 TO 10

Combine the macaroni, mozzarella and provolone cheeses, and the tomato sauce in a bowl and set aside.

Coat a 9-inch springform pan with olive oil spray. Cut a piece of parchment paper to fit the bottom of the pan. Cover the parchment paper with the prosciutto or pancetta slices, overlapping them. Set aside.

Combine the ground meats in a large bowl. Dip the bread slices quickly in a small bowl of water and squeeze out the excess. Crumble the bread over the meats. Add the eggs, basil, parsley, salt and pepper, pecorino cheese, and garlic. Mix gently with your hands to blend the ingredients (the mixture can be prepared and refrigerated a day ahead).

Preheat the oven to 350°F.

Wet your hands and pat about two-thirds of the meat mixture evenly over the prosciutto or pancetta. Be sure to spread the meat to the edges of the pan so there are no gaps.

Carefully spread the macaroni mixture over the meat. Pat it down firmly with your hands or a wooden spoon.

Use a rolling pin to roll out the remaining meat between two sheets of wax paper into a 9½-inch round to fit the top of the pan.

Carefully pull back one sheet of the wax paper and invert the meat over the top of the macaroni mixture. Remove the remaining sheet of wax paper.

Neatly press the meat along the edges of the pan to form a seal.

Cover the pan tightly with aluminum foil. Place the pan on a baking sheet and bake for 40 minutes. Remove the aluminum foil and bake 15 to 20 minutes longer, until the top is nicely browned.

Remove the pan from the oven. Run a knife around the edges of the pan. Let the pan cool for 5 minutes.

Place a round serving platter larger than the pan over the top and invert the casserole onto the platter.

Use a pot holder to release the spring and carefully lift off the sides. Remove the bottom of the pan and the parchment paper.

Serve the timballo cut into wedges and pass extra tomato sauce on the side.

## Ingredients

4 tablespoons olive oil

3 eggplants at least 11-inches long, cut into ¼-inch-thick lengthwise slices

½ cup toasted bread crumbs

### SAUCE

2 tablespoons olive oil

½ cup onions, minced

1 rib celery, minced

1 large carrot, scraped and minced

2 garlic cloves, minced

5 cups chopped fresh or canned plum tomatoes

¼ cup dry red wine

1 bay leaf

Salt and pepper to taste

### FILLING FOR THE MOLD

1 pound ground veal

1 large egg, lightly beaten

2 tablespoons dry white wine

2 tablespoons grated pecorino cheese

½ cup fresh bread crumbs

1 teaspoon salt

2 cups cooked bucatini or spaghetti, broken into thirds

1½ cups fresh mozzarella cheese, cut into bits

¼ cup grated percorino cheese

¼ cup Italian parsley, minced

# Timballo di Melanzane e Bucatini
## EGGPLANT AND BUCATINI CASSEROLE

The movie *Big Night* showcased this eggplant timballo filled with bucatini, (a thick spaghetti with a hole in the center), tiny meatballs, and cubes of cheese. Its origins go deep into the past when these elaborate dishes were prepared for the "upper crust" of southern Italian society. You can make the filling for this impressive dish in stages; it is easy to assemble in a springform pan, and most of the ingredients can be prepped ahead of time. When I make it, smiles are everywhere at the dinner table. And it is a winner on any buffet table.

SERVES 10 TO 12

Preheat the oven to 350°F.

Use 1 tablespoon of olive oil to grease the springform pan. Coat it with bread crumbs and place in the refrigerator (do this step a day ahead).

Brush two or three baking sheets with olive oil and lay the eggplant slices on them in single rows. Bake the slices in batches, about 5 to 7 minutes, or until they begin to brown; they should be soft and pliable, not mushy. Cool the slices.

For the sauce, heat the remaining olive oil in a large saucepan over medium heat. Add the onions, celery, and carrot. Cook, stirring occasionally until the vegetables soften. Stir in the garlic and cook until it begins to soften. Stir in the tomatoes, wine, bay leaf, salt, and pepper. Cover the pan.

Lower the heat to medium-low and cook for 20 minutes. Remove the cover and simmer the sauce for 5 minutes. Set aside. (This step can be done weeks ahead, and the sauce frozen or made 3 or 4 days ahead).

Combine the veal, egg, wine, cheese, parsley, bread crumbs, and salt. Mix just to combine the ingredients. Wet your hands and make marble-size meatballs. Place them on a lightly oiled rimmed baking sheet and bake for about 7 to 10 minutes or until cooked. Transfer the meatballs to a large bowl. (This step can be done two days ahead and refrigerated).

Line and overlap the eggplant slices lengthwise over the sides of the springform pan, leaving about a 3-inch overhang. Do not leave any gaps around the edges of the pan. Line the base of the pan with more slices, and be sure to fill in any gaps with smaller pieces of eggplant.

Add the bucatini to the same bowl as the meatballs. Stir in 2 cups of the tomato sauce and the mozzarella cheese. Combine the mixture well. Spoon the mixture into the pan, packing it in tightly.

Fold the overlapping ends of the eggplant slices in toward the center of the pan, covering the ingredients. Place the pan on a rimmed baking sheet to catch any drips.

Spread ½ cup of tomato sauce over the top of the mold and sprinkle with ¼ cup grated pecorino cheese.

Cover the top tightly with a sheet of aluminum foil and bake for 45 minutes. Uncover the pan and bake an additional 15 minutes.

Remove the pan from the oven and let rest, tented, for 10 to 15 minutes to allow it to firm up before cutting into it.

Run a butter knife along the inside edges of the pan. Release the spring and place the timballo on a flat serving dish. Cut into wedges to serve and pass additional sauce on the side.

> ✿ TIP: A neater cut will be achieved if the casserole is baked and refrigerated a day ahead. When ready to serve, simply reheat the casserole, covered on a baking sheet until it is hot, about 30 minutes, then remove from the oven; let rest for 5 minutes. Release spring and remove pan sides. Place the timballo on a serving dish, cut into thick wedges, and serve with additional tomato sauce on the side.

## PORK SAUSAGE RAGÙ

1 tablespoon extra virgin
    olive oil
1 medium onion, minced
½ pound ground pork
    sausage
6 cups canned plum
    tomatoes
½ cup red wine
Salt and freshly ground
    black pepper to taste
6 or 7 fresh basil leaves

## MEATBALLS

¼ pound ground beef
¼ pound ground pork
½ cup ounces grated
    pecorino cheese
¼ cup soft bread crumbs
2 tablespoons minced
    fresh Italian parsley
1 teaspoon minced garlic
2 eggs
Olive oil for frying
1 pound fresh mozzarella
    cheese, cut into bits
1 pound mezzi ziti or
    bucatini, broken into
    thirds

# Timballo di Mezzi Ziti
## BAKED MACARONI CASSEROLE PUGLIESI STYLE

Pugliesi love their baked macaroni casseroles *(timballi)* and they are standard fare for Christmas or other special occasions. Mezzi ziti are a long, hollow type of dried pasta that need to be broken in thirds before cooking. If they are unavailable use bucatini, a thick, hollow spaghetti. This recipe is usually made in a terra-cotta dish, but any heavy casserole or deep lasagne pan will work.

SERVES 6 TO 8

To make the ragù, heat the olive oil in a 2-quart saucepan; stir in the onion and cook until it is limp. Stir in the sausage and cook until it is browned. Combine the tomatoes with the wine and stir into the sausage mixture. Add salt and pepper to taste. Cook at a simmer, uncovered, for 30 minutes. Stir in the basil. Set aside.

Mix all the ingredients for the meatballs together in a bowl except the olive oil, mozzarella cheese, and mezzi ziti. Make tiny meatballs the size of marbles. Pour a thin layer of olive oil in a sauté pan and fry the meatballs in batches. Or bake the meatballs on a lightly oiled baking sheet at 350°F for 12 minutes. Transfer the meatballs to a large bowl and mix them with 1 cup of the ragù. Set aside.

Cook the mezzi ziti according to the directions on page 53. They should remain just a bit firmer because they will finish cooking in the oven. Drain them and transfer to a bowl. Toss with 1 cup of the sauce and set aside.

Preheat the oven to 350°F.

Spread a thin layer of the ragù in a heavy ovenproof dish. Spread one-third of the mezzi ziti over the sauce. For the next layer, combine the meatballs mixed with half of the cheese and cover the mezzi ziti.

Spread 1 cup of the sauce over the cheese and meatballs. Make a second layer like the first. Spread the remaining mezzi ziti over the second layer and top with the rest of the sauce. Sprinkle the remaining cheese evenly over the entire surface of the casserole.

Bake covered with aluminum foil for 30 minutes, then uncover and bake 10 to 15 minutes or longer. The top should be very crispy.

# Timballo di Pane e Formaggio
## BREAD AND CHEESE CASSEROLE

This unusual timballo uses whole wheat bread. I am particularly fond of it because it is so filling as a main dish and yet can also double as a side dish. The mixture of cheeses creates a creamy texture. Use a tomato knife to cut through the soft cheeses.

SERVES 8

Heat the olive oil in a sauté pan and cook the leeks with the bay leaf over medium heat until the leeks soften. Discard the bay leaf and spread the leeks in the bottom of a 9×12 or 12×2 casserole dish.

Make a single layer of bread slices. Top with a layer of half the mixed cheeses. Top the cheese with a layer of tomatoes. Sprinkle the layer with salt, cinnamon, and nutmeg.

Continue making another layer of bread, cheese, and tomato and end with a bread layer.

Pour the wine over the casserole and drizzle the top with the olive oil.

Bake uncovered for 35 to 40 minutes, until the top is crusty. Allow the timballo to sit for 5 minutes before cutting into pieces.

2 tablespoons olive oil

3 large leeks (white part only), thinly sliced

1 large bay leaf

1 pound thin-sliced whole wheat bread

½ pound Asiago cheese, diced

¼ pound Swiss cheese, diced

¼ pound Italian fontina cheese, cut into small pieces

½ cup grated Parmigiano-Reggiano

4 to 5 large plum tomatoes, thinly sliced

Salt to taste

¼ teaspoon ground cinnamon

Freshly ground nutmeg to taste

1 cup dry white wine

Extra virgin olive oil for drizzling

6 large eggs

Twenty-one ½-inch slices semolina or sourdough bread

Salt and freshly ground black pepper to taste

1 cup milk

¼ pound salame or soppressata, thinly sliced and cut in half

12 ounces scamorza cheese, smoked or unsmoked, coarsely chopped

4 tablespoons (½ stick) butter, cut into bits

# Timballo di Scamorza
## SCAMORZA CHEESE CASSEROLE

Call it a *timpano* or *timballo*, it all comes down to a molded and baked affair that contains ingredients like rice, pasta, potatoes, eggs, or bread as a binder. Naples is famous for its timpano made with thick pasta, tiny meatballs, and peas. Emilia-Romagna is famous for its *bomba*, a type of timpano made with rice, a luscious cream sauce, mushrooms, ham, and exotic truffles. Impressive, yes, and time consuming to make. This simple timballo, made with bread, eggs, cheese, and salami, takes its inspiration from southern Italy and takes minutes to prepare. It can be assembled ahead of time, is perfect as a brunch or buffet offering, and is even good cold as a leftover. Critical to the success of the dish is the quality of the bread; use a good semolina or sourdough type. Scamorza is a mozzarella cheese that is smoked or unsmoked.

SERVES 8

Brush an 8×13×2-inch casserole dish with olive oil and set aside.

Preheat the oven to 350°F.

Crack the eggs into a large bowl and beat them with a whisk until foamy. Whisk in the milk and salt and pepper.

Lay the bread slices in a single layer on each of two rimmed baking sheets.

Divide and pour the egg mixture over the slices and allow them to absorb the mixture.

Use a wide spatula to lift the bread slices and make a single layer of seven slices in the casserole; do not worry if there are gaps. Top with half of the salame and half of the cheese. Make a second layer like the first. Top with the last layer of bread and dot the top with the butter.

Place a sheet of wax paper over the top and press on it with your hands to compress the bread slices. Remove and discard the wax paper.

Bake for 40 to 45 minutes, until the top is nicely browned. Cut into squares and serve hot or at room temperature.

CIAO ITALIA SLOW AND EASY

# Timballo alla Teramano
## CREPES WITH SPINACH AND VEAL, TERAMANO STYLE

For the tenth season of *Ciao Italia* I decided to visit Italian-American neighborhoods across the United States to get an idea of what kinds of Italian comfort foods were still being made at home. I was fortunate to meet chef Anthony Stella, who lives in Wilmington, Delaware, and owns a restaurant called Osteria. Anthony's family is from the Abruzzi region and he still makes gnocchi and *timballo alla Teramano* the way it has been done in that region for decades. This recipe was taught to him by his cousin's wife, Rosalba, who is from Teramo, a large city in the Abruzzi. This timballo sounds like a lot of work to put together but it can be assembled in stages. Anthony's is a little different in that instead of pasta, *crespelle*, or crepes, are layered into the mold. The crepes can be made ahead and refrigerated for several days or frozen for a month as long as they are well wrapped.

SERVES 8 TO 10

Generously grease a 12×10-inch baking dish with butter and sprinkle with bread crumbs. Refrigerate until ready to use.

To make the crepes, in a blender or bowl, combine all the crepe ingredients except for the butter. Cover and allow the batter to rest for 1 hour or overnight. When ready to use, bring to room temperature and whisk in the butter.

Spray a 7-inch Teflon-coated fry pan with vegetable spray. Heat the fry pan and pour about ¼ cup of the batter into the pan. Swirl the pan to coat the bottom and cook the crepe until the edge begins to brown and the crepe is firm to the touch. Invert the pan to remove the crepes as you make them and allow them to cool between sheets of wax paper on a rack lined with a kitchen towel. Continue making crepes until all the batter has been used. There should be about twenty crepes.

For the spinach, cook the onion in a sauté pan in the olive oil until

## CREPES
4 tablespoons (½ stick) unsalted butter, melted
Bread crumbs for sprinkling
3 eggs
¾ cup plus 2 tablespoons milk
¾ cup plus 2 tablespoons seltzer water
1 teaspoon salt
1 cup unbleached all-purpose flour
Vegetable spray

## SPINACH
1 onion, minced
¼ cup extra virgin olive oil
1½ pounds chopped fresh spinach leaves
½ teaspoon freshly grated nutmeg
¼ teaspoon salt
¼ teaspoon freshly ground black pepper

## VEAL
2 pounds ground veal
1 teaspoon salt
1 teaspoon minced garlic
3 tablespoons chopped fresh Italian parsley
¼ cup grated pecorino cheese
2 large eggs, beaten
1 cup bread crumbs

## SAUCE

Two 28-ounce cans whole
plum tomatoes
½ cup extra virgin olive oil
1 onion, cut in half
1 teaspoon light brown
sugar
1 teaspoon ground black
pepper
1 teaspoon kosher salt

## ZUCCHINI

5 large zucchini, trimmed
and cut lengthwise into
¼-inch slices
3 large eggs, beaten
1 cup unbleached all-
purpose flour
1 teaspoon salt
1 cup dried bread crumbs
Peanut oil for deep frying

## ASSEMBLY

1 cup grated pecorino
cheese
4 ounces fresh mozzarella
balls, cut into ½-inch
cubes
6 eggs, slightly beaten
½ cup heavy cream

soft. Add the spinach and the remaining ingredients and cook until most of the liquid has evaporated. Transfer the spinach to a bowl and let it cool.

For the veal, mix all of the veal ingredients together in a bowl and spread the mixture out onto a rimmed cookie sheet to a thickness of about ¼ inch. Bake the veal at 350°F for 30 minutes. Cool the meat and cut it into cubes. Set aside.

For the sauce, pass the tomatoes through a fine screen on a food mill or a sieve. Heat the olive oil in a sauté pan, add the onion halves and tomatoes, and bring the mixture to a rapid boil. Lower the heat and simmer the ingredients until thickened. Season the sauce with the sugar, pepper, and salt. Keep the sauce warm.

For the zucchini, salt the slices and stand them up in a bowl for 1 hour to extract the excess water. Rinse and dry the zucchini. In a bowl combine the eggs and flour. Dip the slices in the egg mixture, then in bread crumbs. Fry the zucchini in batches in hot (375°F) peanut oil.

Drain on paper towels and cut the slices into 1-inch cubes. Set aside.

Preheat the oven to 350°F.

To assemble, begin to fill the baking dish by covering the bottom of the dish with a layer of four crepes, overlapping them as you go. Spread a thin layer of spinach over the crepes followed by a layer of the veal cubes, zucchini, grated pecorino cheese, and the mozzarella. Mix the eggs and cream and add some of the mixture in a layer. Continue making layers of crepes and filling. There should be four layers of filling and five layers of crepes. Be sure to press down each layer with your hands before adding the next one. Cover the top of the crepes with the tomato sauce. Reserve the remaining sauce to pass at the table.

Bake the timballo for 1 hour. Allow it to cool for 15 minutes before cutting. Serve the timballo as is or pass additional tomato sauce.

# Pasticcio di Maccheroni
## SICILIAN-STYLE CHICKEN PIE

Whenever I make *pasticcio di maccheroni,* I think of Giuseppe Lampedusa's novel, *The Leopard,* about the decline of the aristocracy in nineteenth-century Sicily. In his elegantly written book, Lampedusa describes lavish multicourse dinners at which "three lackeys in green, gold, and powder entered, each holding a great silver dish containing a towering macaroni pie." Pasticcio di maccheroni is easy to assemble if you make the slightly sweet dough a day ahead and have some cooked or leftover chicken on hand. Or the entire pie can be assembled in one day, covered with a sheet of buttered parchment paper, and baked the next day. Either way, this savory, deep-dish pie will be the centerpiece of your buffet table.

SERVES 8 TO 10

In a bowl mix together the flour, sugar, salt, and zest. Using a fork or pastry blender, work in the butter until the mixture resembles coarse crumbs.

In a small bowl, whisk together the egg yolks with ½ cup water. Add the yolks to the flour mixture and mix with your hands until a soft dough is formed. If the dough seems dry, add a little water. Gather the dough into a ball. Divide it in half and wrap each piece in plastic wrap. Refrigerate overnight.

For the filling, bring 6 quarts salted water to a boil in a large pot. Add the penne and cook until just al dente; the pasta should remain slightly undercooked. Add the peas to the boiling water during the last 3 minutes of cooking. Drain well and place in a large bowl. Add the cheese and butter and toss well. Set aside.

In another bowl, combine the chicken and chicken broth. Set aside. Preheat the oven to 375°F.

Butter a 10×3-inch springform pan. On a lightly floured surface, roll one piece of dough into a 16-inch round. Fit the dough into the pan, letting the excess hang over the sides.

Place one-third of the pasta mixture in the pastry shell and sprinkle

### DOUGH
2¾ cups unbleached all-purpose flour

¼ cup sugar

½ teaspoon fine sea salt

1 tablespoon grated lemon zest

8 tablespoons (1 stick) butter, cut into pieces and softened

3 large egg yolks

### FILLING
1 pound penne

One 10-ounce package frozen peas, thawed

2 cups grated Asiago cheese

5 tablespoons butter, softened

1¼ pounds cooked chicken, cut into bite-size pieces (about 2½ cups)

1 cup chicken broth

Fine sea salt to taste

1 egg, slightly beaten

with salt. Spread half of the chicken and broth mixture over the pasta. Repeat with another layer of pasta and another layer of chicken. Spread the remaining pasta over the chicken and sprinkle with salt.

On a floured surface, roll out the remaining dough to a 12-inch round. Place the dough over the filling. Trim off the excess dough, leaving a 1-inch overhang, and pinch the edges together to seal. If you wish, reroll the scraps and cut out shapes to make a decorative design on top of the pie. Brush the top of the pie with the beaten egg.

Bake for 45 minutes or until the crust is nicely browned. Transfer the pan to a rack and let cool for 10 minutes for easier cutting. Release the spring on the side of the pan and transfer the pasticcio to a serving plate. With a sharp knife, cut into wedges and serve.

> TIP: The dough can be made two days ahead of time and refrigerated. Use a rotisserie-cooked chicken to save time.

# Poultry
## Casseroles

Anatra alla Nizzarda
(Duck with Olives, Herbs, and
Mushrooms)

Pollo e Fontina
(Chicken and Fontina Cheese
Casserole)

Pollo al Cartoccio
(Chicken Packages)

Pollo alla Ghiotta
(Glutton-Style Chicken)

Fricco di Pollo all'Eugubina
(Gubbian-Style Stewed Chicken)

Pollo Crostoso
(Crusty and Cheesy Chicken Casserole)

Pollo Marengo
(Chicken Marengo)

Pollo in Padella
(Chicken Skillet Supper)

Pollo Tetrazzini
(Chicken Tetrazzini)

Torta di Pollo e Verdure
(Chicken Pot Pie with Vegetables)

Rollato di Tacchino
(Stuffed and Rolled Turkey Breast)

Coniglio in Umido all'Eugubina
(Rabbit Gubbian Style)

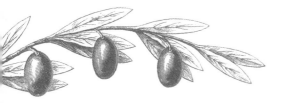

MY FIRST CHOICE WHEN PURCHASING POULTRY IS free range and organic. This means that chickens are allowed to move around freely outdoors and no antibiotics or artificial growth hormones are used. And no artificial ingredients are used in the feed. Organic/free range chickens will cost considerably more, but the difference in taste is quite noticeable. Look for the certified organic label on your selection to ensure that is what you are buying. Inspection of poultry is mandatory by law but grading is not. Poultry is graded according to the USDA Agricultural Marketing Service regulations. Grade A poultry is plump, with meaty bodies, clean skin free of feathers, discoloration, and cuts and bruises.

Any poultry labeled fresh must mean it has never been frozen. Fresh poultry held at 0 degrees or below must be labeled frozen or previously frozen.

Precautions should be taken when handling poultry. Refrigerate raw meat as soon as you get home and never leave it out at room temperature. Keep it in the coldest part of the refrigerator and use it within a day. Defrost poultry in the refrigerator, not at room temperature.

When preparing poultry, use a plastic cutting board or plastic meat sheets found in kitchen stores. Wash hands, countertop, and other areas that raw chicken has come in contact with. It is a good idea to keep a bacterial soap spray handy for cleaning areas exposed to raw poultry.

*Tiella di Cozze*
(Mussel Casserole) pg. 15

*Conchiglioni Ripieni al Forno*
(Large Shells Stuffed with Ragù and Cream) pg. 53

*Frutte di Mare in Padella*
(Seafood Casserole) pg. 10

*Lasagne in Padella ai Carciofi e Formaggio* (Skillet Lasagne with Artichokes and Cheese)
pg. 57

LEFT: *Spezzatelle* (Lamb and Dandelion Casserole) pg. 44

ABOVE: *Pollo al Cartoccio* (Chicken Packages) pg. 81

LEFT: *Prosciutto Cotto con Broccolo e Besciamella* (Ham and Broccoli Casserole in White Sauce) pg. 41

*Bomba di Riso alla Mara*
(Mara's Rice Bomb) pg. 23

*Costine con Rigatoni*
(Sunday Night Beef Short Ribs
with Rigatoni) pg. 33

*Pollo in Padella* (Chicken
Skillet Supper)
pg. 86

*Strati di Verdure Miste (Layered Mixed Vegetable Casserole) pg. 116*

*Timballo di Maccarun*
(Molded Macaroni Casserole) pg. 64

# Anatra alla Nizzarda

## DUCK WITH OLIVES, HERBS, AND MUSHROOMS

Duck dishes always evoke gourmet cooking and this one is no exception. It is said to have originated in Nice, France. Be sure to remove as much fat as possible from the duck so the dish will not be greasy. Niçoise are small, purple-brown olives with a nutty taste. Gaeta olives are a good alternative.

SERVES 4 TO 6

Heat the olive oil and butter in a large stovetop casserole or skillet. Stir in the garlic and allow it to soften, but not brown. When the skillet begins to sizzle, add the duck pieces and brown them. Add the parsley, poultry seasoning, bay leaf, thyme, salt, pepper, and tomatoes. Stir to mix well.

Lower the heat to a simmer and cook for 35 minutes. Uncover the pan, add the wine and Cognac and continue cooking for 25 minutes, stirring occasionally. Add the olives and mushrooms and simmer for another 25 minutes. Correct the seasoning. Serve the duck with some of the sauce on top.

> TIP: Make the dish a day or two ahead and refrigerate. Skim the collected fat from the top of the casserole before reheating.

2 tablespoons olive oil
2 tablespoons butter
1 garlic clove, minced
One 4-pound duck, cut into serving pieces
2 tablespoons minced fresh Italian parsley
1 teaspoon poultry seasoning
1 bay leaf
½ teaspoon minced fresh thyme
1½ teaspoons salt
Freshly ground black pepper (liberal amount)
2 cups chopped plum tomatoes
1 cup dry white wine
⅓ cup Cognac
16 Niçoise or Gaeta olives, pitted
½ pound oyster mushrooms, stemmed and sliced

## Pollo e Fontina

## CHICKEN AND FONTINA CHEESE CASSEROLE

½ cup flour
½ teaspoon salt
Grinding coarse black
    pepper
½ teaspoon grated nutmeg
2 pounds chicken cutlets,
    pounded ¼ inch thick
¾ cup sunflower oil
2 tablespoons butter
½ pound mushrooms,
    stemmed and cut in half
½ pint heavy cream
½ pound Fontina cheese
¼ pound prosciutto di
    Parma cut into 2-inch
    strips
½ cup grated Parmigiano-
    Reggiano cheese
2 tomatoes, sliced into
    rounds

Classic ingredients make this chicken and Fontina cheese casserole a hit every time.

SERVES 6 TO 8

Preheat the oven to 350°F.

Put the flour, salt, pepper, and nutmeg in a plastic bag; close to shake the ingredients together. Add the chicken cutlets a few at a time and dredge them in the flour; shake off the excess. Place the cutlets on a plate and set aside.

Pour the oil into a large sauté pan and heat to medium-high. Brown the cutlets on each side a few at a time. Transfer the cutlets to a large shallow casserole dish. Set aside.

In the same sauté pan, melt the butter and cook the mushrooms until they give off their liquid and begin to brown.

Combine the cream and Fontina cheese in a saucepan over low heat. Stir until the cheese is melted and the sauce is smooth. Cover and set aside.

Sprinkle the mushrooms over the cutlets. Lay the prosciutto strips over the mushrooms and pour the cheese sauce over the top.

Place the tomato slices over the sauce and sprinkle the dish with the Parmigiano-Reggiano cheese.

Bake for 35 to 40 minutes or until the cheese is bubbly browned.

# Pollo al Cartoccio
## CHICKEN PACKAGES

Surprise! Everybody gets an individually wrapped mini chicken casserole flavored with fennel, sage, rosemary, and marjoram. Using the wrapping technique allows the chicken to remain moist and juicy.

SERVES 4

2 tablespoons olive oil

2 tablespoons butter

5 large fresh sage leaves

2 tablespoons fresh rosemary leaves

1 tablespoon fresh marjoram

Salt and freshly ground black pepper to taste

8 pieces cut-up chicken (about 3 pounds)

1 large fennel bulb, cut in half, each half cut into 4 chunks

8 thin slices prosciutto di Parma

Preheat the oven to 350°F.

Heat the olive oil and butter in a small saucepan until the butter is melted.

Finely chop the sage, rosemary, and marjoram together and transfer them to a small bowl. Stir in the olive oil and butter. Season with salt and pepper and mix very well.

Brush four sheets of parchment paper or aluminum foil with olive oil. Using a pastry brush, coat each piece of chicken with the herb-butter mixture.

Wrap each piece of chicken along with a chunk of fennel in a slice of prosciutto di Parma.

Lay two pieces of the wrapped chicken on one end of each of the four sheets of parchment paper or aluminum foil. Fold the other end over the chicken and fold the edges and sides over several times on themselves to seal the package.

Place the packages in a single layer in a large casserole dish.

Bake for 45 minutes or until a knife is easily inserted into the chicken and the juices run clear.

Remove the casserole from the oven and allow it to stand for 5 minutes. Place a packet on each of four dinner plates. Use scissors to cut from the center of the paper or aluminum foil outward in four directions, making a cross. Fold the four corners back to serve.

# Pollo alla Ghiotta

## GLUTTON-STYLE CHICKEN

One 3½-pound chicken,
 cut into serving pieces
6 tablespoons unsalted
 butter
1 cup dry white wine
1 cup whole milk
1 cup tomato juice or
 vegetable juice
Salt and freshly ground
 black pepper to taste

*Alla ghiotta* means glutton, but here it refers to a cooking style in which a sauce is created from several liquids. For this tasty chicken dish, it is milk, tomato juice, and white wine.

Everything goes in the pot at once and simmers nicely with an occasional stir.

SERVES 4 TO 6

Place all the ingredients in a skillet or stovetop casserole and simmer uncovered, stirring occasionally for 35 to 40 minutes, until fork tender. Correct the seasoning.

VARIATION: add chopped carrots, celery, onions, and green beans.

# Fricco di Pollo all'Eugubina

## GUBBIAN-STYLE STEWED CHICKEN

A *fricco* is a stew of sorts, and in this easy to prepare Gubbian-style chicken stew, it is Orvieto Classico wine that gives great merit to its flavor along with the presence of rosemary, which shows the fondness that Umbrians have for this herb in many of their foods. This dish is even better if made the day before serving.

SERVES 4

¼ cup extra virgin olive oil
1 large white onion,
    coarsely chopped
3½ pounds cut-up bone-in
    chicken, dried well with
    paper towels
¼ cup white wine vinegar
1 cup Orvieto Classico or
    other dry white wine
4 large plum tomatoes,
    pureed and sieved to
    remove skin and seeds
Fine sea salt to taste
Coarsely ground black
    pepper to taste
4 fresh sage leaves,
    shredded
2 fresh rosemary sprigs

Heat the olive oil in a large sauté pan and cook the onion over medium-low heat until it is soft and translucent. Raise the heat to medium-high and add the chicken pieces. Be sure they are dried well.

Brown well on all sides. This should take about 5 minutes. Add the vinegar and allow it to evaporate. Lower the heat and continue cooking for 15 minutes.

Raise the temperature to high, add the wine, and allow it to evaporate. Pour in the pureed tomato. Season the mixture with salt and pepper, add the sage and rosemary, and continue cooking uncovered for 25 minutes or until the juices thicken and the chicken is tender when pierced with a fork.

Arrange the chicken on a platter; pour the sauce over the top.

1 tablespoon olive oil

1 medium onion, coarsely chopped

1 cup diced celery

1 teaspoon celery seed

Sea salt to taste

1 rotisserie-cooked whole chicken (about 3 pounds), meat removed from the bone and cut into 1-inch chunks

One 16-ounce package fresh spinach, stemmed, washed, drained, and torn into pieces

**SAUCE**

3 tablespoons butter

3 tablespoons unbleached all-purpose flour

4 cups low-fat milk

Freshly grated nutmeg

Salt to taste

2 cups grated Asiago cheese

# Pollo Crostoso

## CRUSTY AND CHEESY CHICKEN CASSEROLE

Really pressed for time? Use a rotisserie-cooked whole chicken found in your supermarket for this crusty chicken and Asiago cheese–topped casserole.

SERVES 4

Preheat the oven to 350°F.

Heat the olive oil in an ovenproof casserole and cook the onion and celery until softened. Transfer the mixture to a large bowl and stir in the celery seed, salt, chicken, and spinach. Set aside.

In the same casserole, melt the butter over medium heat and whisk in the flour; whisk until the mixture forms a smooth paste. Slowly whisk in the milk. Continue whisking until the mixture comes to a boil and begins to thicken. Do not make the sauce too thick. It should be the consistency of pancake batter. Stir in the nutmeg and salt.

Combine the chicken mixture with the sauce.

Cover the pan and bake the casserole for 25 to 30 minutes. Uncover and sprinkle the cheese evenly over the top. Bake 5 to 8 minutes longer, just until the cheese begins to bubble and brown.

---

TIP: It is easier to separate the meat from the bones while the chicken is still warm.

# Pollo Marengo
## CHICKEN MARENGO

Like the Chicken Tetrazzini recipe on page 87, this one for chicken Marengo also has a story behind it. Marengo is a city south of Turin in the Piedmont region of Italy where Napoleon defeated the Austrians in 1800. Not in the habit of eating before a battle, he was starving after the victory and commanded his chef, Dumand, to whip something up. Desperate for ingredients, Dumand send foragers out to search for food and what materialized was a scrawny chicken, a few crayfish, a handful of tomatoes, some eggs, garlic, and a frying pan. Dumand got to work. What he created left Napoleon begging for more, and so he ordered that after each battle, this dish must be served! I must beg Napoleon's forgiveness for not including crayfish in the recipe, but if available, they are added as a fried garnish on top of the dish. Dumand tried to improve this dish by adding mushrooms, but Napoleon, being highly superstitious, associated the original recipe with victory, so no substitutions could be made!

SERVES 6

¼ cup unbleached all-purpose flour
1 teaspoon salt
½ teaspoon black pepper
One 3½-pound chicken, cut into pieces
¼ cup olive oil
1 onion, chopped
1 garlic clove, minced
1 cup fresh or canned chopped tomatoes
¼ cup sherry or white wine
4 fried eggs for garnish (optional)

Place the flour, salt, and pepper in a paper bag. Add the chicken pieces a few at a time and shake in the closed bag to coat with flour. Transfer the pieces to a dish.

Heat the olive oil in a cast iron skillet or stovetop casserole dish. Brown the chicken a few pieces at a time and set aside.

Sauté the onion in the same pan until it softens; stir in the garlic and continue to cook until the garlic is soft. Return the chicken to the pan along with the tomatoes and sherry. Cover and cook over low heat for 30 to 40 minutes, until the chicken is fork tender.

Meanwhile, fry the eggs one at a time and place one on each plate as a garnish.

## Pollo in Padella

### CHICKEN SKILLET SUPPER

2 tablespoons pine nuts

1½ teaspoons fine sea salt

½ teaspoon coarsely
ground black pepper

1 tablespoon dried
oregano

1 teaspoon celery salt

½ teaspoon hot red
pepper flakes

3 pounds cut-up chicken
pieces, washed and
dried

3 tablespoons olive oil

2 tablespoons lemon juice

1 medium onion, chopped

3 small red-skin potatoes,
cut into quarters

½ cup prepared tomato
sauce (page 99)

1 cup chicken broth or dry
white wine

1 teaspoon sugar

½ pound green beans, cut
into thirds

*Pollo in padella* is a dish that is requested often at my dinner table. The secret to its great flavor is a simple dry rub of salt, pepper, oregano, celery salt, and red pepper flakes.

SERVES 4

Toast the pine nuts in a small nonstick sauté pan over medium heat until they are fragrant and lightly browned. Transfer to a dish.

Combine the salt, pepper, oregano, celery salt, and pepper flakes in a small bowl. Mix well, then rub evenly over the chicken pieces.

Heat the oil in a large heavy sauté pan or cast iron skillet over medium-high heat.

Brown the chicken pieces skin side down a few at a time if necessary. Do not crowd the pan or the chicken will steam instead of brown. Add the lemon juice and ⅓ cup water, cover the pan, and simmer for 30 minutes, turning the pieces every 10 minutes.

Transfer the chicken to a platter and set aside. Add the onion and potatoes to the pan; increase the heat to medium-high and sauté for 3 minutes. Stir in the tomato sauce, chicken broth or wine, and sugar. Bring to a boil, stirring frequently. Stir in the beans and return the chicken to the pan.

Cover and simmer over medium heat for about 10 minutes, until the beans are tender. Serve with some of the sauce and a sprinkling of pine nuts over the top.

# Pollo Tetrazzini
## CHICKEN TETRAZZINI

Do you remember chicken Tetrazzini? This classic casserole made with mushrooms, spaghetti, and a velvet cream sauce was popular in the 1950s but seems to have disappeared. It was created by an Italian chef in honor of Luisa Tetrazzini (1871–1940), the opera singer whose role as Violetta in *La Traviata* made her a star; she could hit high notes like no one else in her day. And you'll be singing your own praises of this updated tasty classic.

SERVES 6 TO 8

5 tablespoons butter

2 tablespoons olive oil

1 pound sliced button, shiitake, or oyster mushrooms, or a mix

¼ cup flour

2 cups hot low-sodium chicken broth

1 cup heavy cream or nonfat half-and-half

3 tablespoons fresh lemon juice

Salt and freshly ground black pepper to taste

¼ teaspoon freshly grated nutmeg

½ pound spaghetti, cooked

3 cups diced cooked chicken

⅔ cup grated Parmigiano-Reggiano cheese

Preheat the oven to 350°F.

Melt 2 tablespoons of the butter and the olive oil in a large, 2½-quart stovetop casserole dish or ovenproof sauté pan. Cook the mushrooms over medium heat until they soften, 6 to 8 minutes. Transfer them to a bowl.

Melt the remaining butter in the same pan and whisk in the flour to make a smooth paste. Slowly pour in the chicken broth and cook, whisking constantly, until the mixture just begins to thicken. Whisk in the half-and-half or cream and continue whisking until the sauce thickens; stir in the lemon juice. Season with salt, pepper, and nutmeg.

Mix the spaghetti, chicken, and mushrooms into the sauce.

Sprinkle the cheese over the top and bake uncovered for 30 to 35 minutes, until the chicken is heated through and the cheese is nicely browned.

> TIPS: Don't be in a hurry to stir the mushrooms as they cook; let them begin to exude their water and brown before turning them.
>
> Use a store-bought rotisserie-cooked chicken for the recipe if pressed for time.

## Torta di Pollo e Verdure

### CHICKEN POT PIE WITH VEGETABLES

1½ pounds boneless, skinless, split chicken breasts

½ cups cooked arborio rice (½ cup raw)

8 ounces whole milk ricotta cheese, well drained

¼ cup milk

4 eggs, beaten

2 cups shredded provolone cheese (about 8 ounces)

¼ cup chopped onion

½ cup chopped red bell pepper

¼ cup chopped fresh Italian parsley

2 tablespoons minced fresh basil

1 teaspoon dried oregano

½ teaspoon hot red pepper flakes

Salt and freshly ground black pepper to taste

1 small zucchini, shredded

1 cup toasted bread crumbs

Think of a classic chicken pot pie without the crust when making this casserole that is perfect for a Sunday night supper, company, or as part of a buffet. Arborio rice is Italian short-grain rice used to make risotto; if it is unavailable, use long-grain rice.

SERVES 8 TO 10

Preheat the oven to 350°F.

Lightly coat the bottom and sides of a 9-inch springform pan with oil or cooking spray. Set aside. Place the chicken in a single layer in a large saucepan and add enough water to cover by ½ inch. Bring to a boil, reduce the heat to a simmer, cover, and poach for 12 to 15 minutes, until the chicken is no longer pink inside. Drain and set aside to cool. Cook the rice in 1 cup of water.

In a large bowl beat the ricotta cheese until smooth. Beat in the milk and eggs until well combined. Cut the cooled chicken into bite-size pieces, making about 2 cups. Add the chicken, rice, cheese, onion, bell pepper, parsley, basil, oregano, pepper flakes, salt, pepper, and zucchini to the egg mixture. Blend well.

Pour the chicken mixture into the pan and place it on a baking sheet.

Bake for 1 hour. Scatter the bread crumbs over the top and continue baking for 10 to 12 minutes, until the bread crumbs are golden brown and the center is firm.

Cool slightly, place on a serving dish, then remove the sides and bottom of the springform pan. Serve warm.

# Rollato di Tacchino
## STUFFED AND ROLLED TURKEY BREAST

Thanksgiving is my favorite holiday. I am in the kitchen many days before the holiday, making preparations so the celebration dinner runs as smoothly as possible. On our table, traditional turkey has given way to a butterflied and stuffed turkey breast, prepared the way Italians like to have it in Perugia, the capital of the region of Umbria. The beauty of this recipe is that it can be made two days ahead and reheated. No hassle, no bones, no mess. A cook can enjoy!

SERVES 8

⅔ pound chestnuts
½ cup olive oil
1½ cups fresh bread crumbs
¼ pound prosciutto, diced
¼ cup fresh rosemary leaves
3 tablespoons chopped fresh Italian parsley leaves
2 large garlic cloves, minced
⅓ cup grated Parmigiano-Reggiano cheese
One 4-pound boneless turkey breast, butterflied
Fine sea salt to taste
Coarsely ground black pepper to taste
1½ cups dry white wine

Preheat the oven to 450°F.

With a small knife, make an X in the top of each chestnut and place the nuts on a baking sheet. Roast for about 25 minutes, until the skins split. Remove and let cool.

Crack the chestnuts open with a nutcracker and remove the nutmeats. Coarsely chop the nutmeats and place in a large bowl. You can, as a time-saver, use jarred or frozen chestnuts that have already been cooked and peeled.

In a skillet, heat ¼ cup of the olive oil. Add the bread crumbs and brown them. Stir in the chestnuts. Transfer the mixture to a bowl.

Add 1 more tablespoon of the oil to the skillet and sauté the prosciutto until crispy. Add to the bread crumb mixture along with the rosemary, parsley, garlic, cheese, and another tablespoon of the oil and mix well. (The stuffing can be covered and refrigerated for up to 2 days.)

To butterfly the turkey breast, use a sharp knife to cut horizontally along the long side of the breast to the other side, but not all the way, so that the meat opens to lie flat like a book. Or ask your butcher to do this for you.

Lay the turkey breast out flat on a cutting board. Place a large piece of wax paper over the turkey and pound it with a meat pounder to flatten it to a ½-inch even thickness. Rub the turkey with salt and pepper. Spread the stuffing mixture evenly over the turkey breast to within an

1 inch of the edges. Do not worry if all of the stuffing does not fit; save any excess for topping the breast after it is rolled.

Starting at one long side, roll the turkey up like a jelly roll and tie it with string in four or five places.

Lower the oven temperature to 350°F.

Heat the remaining 2 tablespoons olive oil in a large skillet over medium-high heat. Brown the turkey roll on all sides. Place the roll on a meat rack in a roasting pan and add the pan juices from the skillet. Sprinkle with salt and pepper and pat any remaining stuffing over the top.

Add ½ cup of the wine to the pan. Roast about 2 hours, until the internal temperature registers between 175° and 180°F on a meat thermometer. Baste the meat occasionally with the pan juices, adding the remaining 1 cup wine to the pan halfway through the cooking time.

Let the meat rest for 15 minutes before slicing it. Then cut the roll into 1-inch-thick slices. Arrange them on a platter and pour any pan juices over the meat. Serve hot or warm.

> TIP: Italian chestnuts appear in stores just in time for Thanksgiving; look for plump, shiny ones that feel heavy in your hand. Avoid buying those that are split or appear wrinkled.

# Coniglio in Umido all'Eugubina
## RABBIT GUBBIAN STYLE

From Gubbio in the region of Umbria comes this succulent rabbit dish traditionally cooked in terra-cotta pots that are presoaked in water for fifteen minutes. The pot absorbs the water through its walls and helps keep the meat moist during cooking. You can achieve good results by using a heavy-duty cast iron casserole or skillet.

SERVES 6

3 pounds rabbit, cut into serving pieces
3 sage leaves, cut into thin strips
1 sprig rosemary, needles only, coarsely chopped
2 garlic cloves, minced
Fine sea salt to taste
Grinding course black pepper
½ cup extra virgin olive oil
2 cups dry white wine
1 cup chicken or vegetable broth

Preheat the oven to 325°F.

Place the rabbit pieces in a casserole dish.

In a bowl mix the sage leaves, rosemary, garlic, salt, and pepper together and rub it all over the rabbit pieces. Mix the olive oil, wine, and broth together and pour over the rabbit. Set aside and marinate for 10 minutes.

Cover the dish and bake for 40 minutes.

Uncover the casserole and raise the heat to 350°F. Cook another 45 minutes or until the rabbit is fork tender and the liquid almost completely absorbed.

Variation: Add sliced potatoes to the bottom of the casserole. The rabbit juices will give a wonderful taste to the potatoes.

# Common Sauces

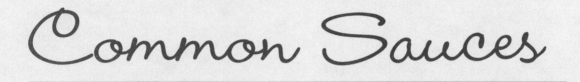

## Salsa di Besciamella
(Basic White Sauce)

## Salsa di Pomodoro
(Tomato Sauce)

## Salsa di Formaggio
(Classic Cheese Sauce)

SAUCES FREQUENTLY USED IN CASSEROLES ARE TO-
mato, milk, cheese, wine, fish, mushroom, and broth based. I always have broths and tomato sauce in the freezer, so all I have to do
when making casseroles that call for these is to defrost them, which
saves me a lot of time.

Cheese sauces are versatile for pasta, vegetables, poultry, and fish-
based casseroles. Think where macaroni and cheese would be if not for
a velvety cheesy sauce? Vary the taste of cheese sauces with the type of
cheese used. See page xiv–xvi for a list of cheeses that work well for
cheese sauces.

Basic tomato sauce (often referred to as marinara) is called for in
many of the recipes in this book and can be made in just 10 to 15 minutes with either fresh or canned plum tomatoes. Tomato sauce is the
perfect partner for pasta dishes, and those with beef or pork. Vary
tomato sauces by adding milk or cream, and herbs such as basil, Italian

parsley, and oregano. The beauty of a basic tomato sauce is that it can be made ahead and frozen for months.

White sauce, known as *besciamella,* is made with milk, either whole or skim, and can have added spices like nutmeg, or herbs like parsley and basil. Add herbs at the end of the cooking process to help them retain their taste and color. White sauces can be made a few days ahead and refrigerated; they do not freeze well.

Wine-based sauces can be made with meat drippings, tomato paste, herbs, and butter or olive oil. Whenever I make a roast, I save any leftover meat juices and drippings and freeze them in containers for use in creating sauces when I need them.

# Salsa di Besciamella
## BASIC WHITE SAUCE

*Besciamella,* or white sauce, is most often associated with northern Italian cooking and is used in oven-baked pasta dishes like lasagne, or with vegetables or fish. It can be made ahead and refrigerated for 3 or 4 days but will thicken as it sits. As you reheat it, thin the sauce with a little milk. The basic recipe does not have added herbs or spices. Those ingredients should be added after the sauce is cooked and should be tailored to the dish being prepared.

MAKES 4 CUPS

8 tablespoons (1 stick) unsalted butter
½ cup unbleached all-purpose flour
4 cups hot milk
Fine sea salt to taste
White pepper to taste

Melt the butter over medium-low heat in a 1½-quart saucepan; do not let the butter brown. Whisk the flour into the butter and cook until a uniform paste is formed and no streaks of flour remain. Slowly whisk in the milk. Cook for about 10 minutes, stirring slowly until the sauce coats the back of a wooden spoon. Season with salt and pepper. Add herbs if desired.

> ✄ TIP: Adding the milk hot will prevent bringing down the temperature of the other ingredients.

4 tablespoons (½ stick)
　　unsalted butter
¼ cup unbleached all-
　　purpose flour
2 cups hot milk
1 cup grated cheese such
　　as Asiago or
　　Parmigiano-Reggiano
Salt to taste

# Salsa di Formaggio
## CLASSIC CHEESE SAUCE

Cheese sauce is very easy to make; it can be made ahead and refrigerated, then reheated and thinned down with a little milk before being added to recipes.

MAKES 2½ CUPS

Melt the butter over medium heat in a 1-quart saucepan; whisk in the flour until a smooth paste is formed. Slowly whisk in the milk and continue whisking over medium heat until the mixture thickens enough to coat a spoon. Off the heat, stir in the cheese.

　　Taste for saltiness.

　　Use immediately or refrigerate covered for up to 4 days.

> TIP: The recipe easily doubles.

# Salsa di Pomodoro
## TOMATO SAUCE

Plum tomatoes, San Marzano varieties from the region of Campania, are best for making tomato sauce because they are meaty and pulpy with few seeds. When not in season, canned San Marzano varieties are available in your grocery store. Tomato sauce is one of the staple ingredients I always have on hand. The sauce freezes beautifully.

MAKES 9½ TO 10 CUPS

5 pounds ripe plum tomatoes or three 28-ounce cans crushed plum tomatoes with their liquid
½ cup extra virgin olive oil
⅔ cup diced onion
3 garlic cloves, minced
1½ cups dry red wine
¼ cup sugar
1 tablespoon fine sea salt or to taste
Freshly ground black pepper to taste
6 to 8 large sprigs fresh basil

If using fresh tomatoes, core them, cut into coarse chunks, and puree in a food processor, blender, or food mill until smooth. Strain the fresh or canned tomatoes through a fine sieve to remove skins and seeds. Set aside.

Heat the olive oil in a large pot and cook the onion over medium heat, stirring, until soft.

Add the garlic and cook, stirring occasionally, until it becomes soft. Do not let the garlic brown or an acid taste will be imparted to the sauce. Add the remaining ingredients, reduce the heat to low, and simmer until thickened, about 15 minutes.

# Veritable Vegetable
## *Casseroles*

Carciofi con Patate al Forno
(Artichoke and Potato Casserole)

Peperoni Rossi alla Napoletano
(Neapolitan-Style Stuffed Red Bell
Peppers)

Manasta Patan alla Nonna Galasso
(Grandma Galasso's Spinach and
Potato Casserole)

Musaka alla Maria
(Maria's Eggplant and Potato Casserole)

Peperonata
(Mixed Bell Pepper Casserole)

Finocchio al Forno in Salsa
Bianca
(Baked Fennel in White Sauce)

La Casseruola di Cipolla da
Cannara
(Onion Casserole from Cannara)

Polpettone di Patata all'Osteria
Luchin
(Osteria Luchin's Potato Meat Loaf)

Rossolare la Casseruola di Riso
Basmati con le Verdure
(Brown Basmati Rice Casserole with
Saucy Vegetables)

Strati di Verdure Miste
(Layered Mixed Vegetable Casserole)

Polenta con Verdure
(Polenta and Vegetable Casserole)

Radicchiella Gratinata
(Crunchy Bread Crumb–Topped
Dandelion Casserole)

Tiella di Verdure
(Pugliesi Vegetable Casserole)

Tortiera di Patate, Pomodori e
Cipolle
(Potato, Tomato, and Onion Casserole)

Tortino di Carciofi
(Sardinian Artichoke Casserole)

Zucchine e Pomodori
(Zucchini and Tomato Casserole)

Ciambotta
(Vegetable Stew)

Zuppa di Val d'Aosta
(Cabbage Casserole from the Val
d'Aosta)

THE TOMATO DEFINES ITALIAN CUISINE MORE THAN any other vegetable, and it was the tomato that put Italy on the international gastronomic map. Scientifically speaking, the tomato is a fruit but its usage in Italian regional cooking has always been that of a vegetable. Without the tomato, pasta would just be a naked dish of bland noodles, many casseroles would lose their character, and Naples would never have created pizza Margherita.

But as much as the tomato is revered, there are many wonderful vegetables that make up the Italian diet; other favorites include eggplant, zucchini, broccoli, cauliflower, fava beans, green beans, onions, leeks, carrots, potatoes, peppers, fennel, artichokes, and—well, the list goes on.

Italians prefer fresh vegetables and very rarely use frozen varieties. They treat their preparation simply, mainly grilling them or sautéeing them quickly in olive oil. They marinate them for antipasti, use them raw in salads, and make them the basis for soups, sauces, fillings, and casseroles. And some vegetables were just meant for casseroles, especially carrots, onions, celery, and garlic, which are considered by Italians to be *"gli odori,"* the underlying flavor agents responsible for unifying flavor.

Vegetable casseroles are some of the easiest to make because most of the ingredients are always on hand. Even vegetables that are not at their prime and have been forgotten in the back of the refrigerator are good in casseroles because they will be baked, so crispness is not an issue.

It is no wonder that the Italian food pyramid is the one to emulate, with its heavy emphasis on vegetables and grains.

# Carciofi con Patate al Forno
## ARTICHOKE AND POTATO CASSEROLE

This artichoke and potato casserole has company written all over it. It is a dish inspired by my Sicilian heritage. Sicilians love artichokes and deftly prepare them in unique ways: baked stuffed with bread crumbs and cheese, slowly stewed (in umido) with tomatoes and onions, fried so their leaves are as crisp as potato chips, and roasted in hot embers right on the ground! Artichokes take a little fussing to clean and prepare. When you purchase them, the leaves should be tightly closed with uniform color and squeak when rolled under your hand. This is an indication that moisture is present and the artichoke is not old. Odd as it may seem, artichokes have an even better flavor if they have been nipped by a frost. Need to save time? Use frozen artichoke hearts instead of fresh.

SERVES 6

4 medium artichokes or one 9-ounce package frozen artichoke hearts, thawed
4 cups water
1½ pounds baking potatoes, peeled and cut into thin rounds
Salt to taste
¼ teaspoon white pepper
2½ cups milk or light cream
⅔ cup grated pecorino cheese

If using fresh artichokes, cut stem ends and remove the outer two layers of leaves and discard them. Cut the artichoke horizontally ½ inch from the top and discard the leaves. If using frozen hearts, cut them into thin slices and set aside.

Place the fresh artichokes in a deep pan large enough to hold them snugly. Pour in enough water to cover them. Bring the artichokes to a boil, then lower the heat and cook them covered until you can easily pull away a leaf, about 30 minutes. Drain the artichokes and allow them to cool.

Remove the remaining leaves (save them to nibble on). Use a spoon to carefully remove the hairy choke in the center. You are now left with the artichoke heart. Clean all the artichokes, then cut the hearts into thin slices.

Toss the potatoes in a bowl with salt and pepper.

Preheat the oven to 350°F.

Lightly butter a 14 × 2½-inch casserole dish or au gratin pan. Make a layer of potatoes in the dish, overlapping them slightly. Arrange half of the artichoke heart slices over the potatoes; sprinkle the layer with salt and pepper, then make another layer like the first, ending with the potatoes.

Slowly pour the milk or cream over the potatoes. Cover the dish with aluminum foil and bake for 45 minutes. Uncover the dish and sprinkle the cheese over the top and bake for an additional 15 minutes or until the cheese has browned slightly. Serve immediately.

---

✻ TIPS: A melon baller or a grapefruit spoon easily removes the hairy choke.

Do not use aluminum pans to cook artichokes, as the metal will leave an off taste. Use porcelain or stainless steel.

Prevent artichokes from tipping over while cooking by wedging a whole potato between them to keep them upright.

---

# Peperoni Rossi alla Napoletano
## NEAPOLITAN-STYLE STUFFED RED BELL PEPPERS

This recipe reflects all that is great about the local products of the region of Campania, particularly Naples, where sweet bell peppers as big as melons grow in the rich volcanic soil around Mount Vesuvius. Add eggplant, another local, rich crop, artisan mozzarella cheese, fragrant basil, and plum tomatoes and you have a history of Neapolitan food in this delicious stuffed sweet pepper casserole.

SERVES 8

8 large red bell peppers
¼ to ½ cup peanut oil
2 small eggplants, peeled and diced
½ cup finely chopped, pitted oil-cured olives
1 tablespoon capers in brine, rinsed and drained
¼ cup finely chopped fresh basil
¼ to ½ cup plus 2 tablespoons extra virgin olive oil
Ten ½-inch slices Italian bread
1 cup diced mozzarella cheese (about ¼ pound)
6 fresh plum tomatoes, chopped
1 cup toasted fresh bread crumbs
½ cup grated Parmigiano-Reggiano cheese

Place the peppers on an oiled grill or broiler pan and grill or broil them, turning them occasionally, until they are blackened all over. Place them in a paper bag, close the bag, and let them cool. Peel off the skins. Remove the core, cut down one side of each pepper, and open them out flat. Carefully brush out the seeds with paper towels and set the peppers aside.

In a skillet, heat ¼ cup of the peanut oil and fry the eggplants in batches until browned, adding more oil as necessary. Remove the eggplants to a large bowl. Add the olives, capers, and basil and mix well.

Wipe out the skillet and add ¼ cup of the olive oil. Heat the oil and fry the bread slices a few at a time, adding more oil as necessary, until browned on both sides. Drain on brown paper. Tear the bread into small pieces and add to the eggplant mixture. Add the cheese and plum tomatoes and mix well.

Preheat the oven to 350°F.

Combine the bread crumbs and Parmigiano-Reggiano cheese.

Place about ½ cup of the eggplant mixture on one end of each pepper and roll each pepper up like a jelly roll. Place the peppers in an oiled baking dish and drizzle them with the 2 tablespoons olive oil. Sprinkle the bread crumb mixture over the top. Bake for 15 minutes or until heated through. This dish can be made a couple of days ahead of time and reheated.

## Manasta Patan alla Nonna Galasso
## GRANDMA GALASSO'S SPINACH AND POTATO CASSEROLE

1 pound spinach, stemmed and washed

½ teaspoon freshly grated nutmeg

2 large all-purpose potatoes, peeled and diced

4 tablespoons (½ stick) butter, melted

1 teaspoon salt and freshly ground black pepper to taste

½ cup plain yogurt (preferably Greek style)

½ cup grated Parmigiano-Reggiano cheese or Italian fontina cut into small bits

Side dishes can be considered casseroles, too. Case in point, *manasta patan,* dialect for spinach and potatoes, was constantly prepared by my maternal grandmother. It was served alone as a main course, but as the recipe was passed from generation to generation, it became a side dish to be served with fish, chicken, or meats. Even now, years later, I am still tweaking this recipe by adding plain Greek yogurt to give it added richness and taste.

SERVES 4 TO 6

Preheat the oven to 350° F.

Steam the spinach in a sauté pan with 2 tablespoons water over medium heat until it has wilted; this will take just a minute or two at most. Drain and squeeze the spinach dry. Chop it and transfer to a medium bowl. Stir in the nutmeg.

Place the potatoes in a 1-quart saucepan and cover with water; add the salt and bring the potatoes to a boil; cook them until they are tender. Drain in a colander.

Transfer the potatoes to a bowl and mash them with a potato masher; do not use a food processor or blender, as this will make the potatoes break down and become very pasty and glue-like. Add the butter, and salt and pepper to taste, and transfer the mixture to the bowl with the spinach; stir in the yogurt and cheese.

Spread the mixture in an oiled pie plate and bake for 35 minutes until bubbly. Serve hot.

# Musaka alla Maria

## MARIA'S EGGPLANT AND POTATO CASSEROLE

Originally Greek in origin, the recipe for this velvety eggplant and potato casserole with two sauces was given to me by a friend from Naples. Called moussaka or *musaka* (an Arabic word), the key ingredient is eggplant. Given that Naples was once a domain of the Greeks, it is safe to say that this dish is transcultural. Other versions of musaka contain ground lamb or beef.

SERVES 6 TO 8

Melt the butter over medium heat in a 2-quart saucepan. Whisk in the flour until well blended. Lower the heat and whisk in the milk. Add the salt, raise the heat to medium-high, and cook, stirring until the sauce has thickened. Cover and set aside. (If you want, make the sauce a day ahead of time and refrigerate it.) Thin it with a little milk if it has thickened too much and reheat over low heat before assembling the musaka.

Place the potatoes in a saucepan and add water to cover. Bring to a boil and cook until the potatoes are tender. Drain and let cool, then peel and thinly slice them. Set aside.

Layer the eggplant in a large pot, sprinkling each layer with salt. Cover and cook the eggplant over low heat for about 5 minutes, just until it begins to get soft. Remove the lid and cook for another 10 minutes. Drain in a colander and set aside.

Preheat the oven to 350°F.

Spread a thin layer of the white sauce in an 11×8-inch casserole dish or baking dish. Add a layer of eggplant and a thin layer of tomato sauce. Sprinkle on a little of the grated cheese and add a layer of potatoes. Cover with another layer of white sauce and continue layering, ending with a layer of potatoes covered with white sauce and sprinkled with cheese.

Bake for 25 to 35 minutes, until the sauce is bubbly and the top has browned. Let sit for 10 minutes before scooping out or cutting into squares.

**WHITE SAUCE**
5 tablespoons butter
¼ cup plus 2 tablespoons all-purpose unbleached flour
4 cups milk
1½ teaspoons fine sea salt

1 pound red-skin potatoes (about 4 medium)
1 eggplant (about 1¼ pounds), sliced into ¼-inch-thick rounds
Fine sea salt to taste
2 cups prepared tomato sauce (page 99)
⅔ cup freshly grated pecorino cheese

2½ pounds mixed red and
   yellow bell peppers
1 pound small white
   onions, peeled
½ cup olive oil
1 pound fresh plum
   tomatoes, seeded and
   quartered
Salt to taste

# *Peperonata*
## MIXED BELL PEPPER CASSEROLE

*Peperonata* is a colorful casserole that originated in the south of Italy, where the climate is just right for growing *peperoni*, or bell peppers. Juicy and sweet, this dish combines red and yellow peppers with small boiling onions and fresh tomatoes. This is a simple and unassuming dish that benefits from time spent choosing the best peppers, onions, and tomatoes.

SERVES 6

Use a preheated outdoor grill to char the peppers, or preheat the broiler and place the peppers on a broiler pan, 3 inches away from the broiler element. Turn them occasionally until the skin is blackened all over. Place them in a paper bag, close the bag, and let them cool.

Remove the skin and core and wipe the seeds out of the peppers with a paper towel.

Cut the peppers into strips. Set aside.

Put the onions in a small pot and cover with water. Bring to a boil and cook for 5 minutes. Drain the onions and set aside.

Heat the olive oil in a cast iron or similar stovetop casserole. Cook the peppers slowly in the oil for 2 minutes; add the onions and tomatoes. Season with salt and cook the mixture until it begins to thicken, for 20 to 25 minutes. Serve hot.

# Finocchio al Forno in Salsa Bianca
## BAKED FENNEL IN WHITE SAUCE

Finocchio, or fennel, is still the "great unknown" Italian vegetable in American markets. This crunchy and licorice-tasting vegetable, similar to celery in texture, has an important place in Italian cooking. Long thought to have medicinal properties, it is still eaten raw as a *digestivo* after meals. Disguise it as a casserole with a simple white sauce and fennel develops a velvety sweet taste that marries well as a side dish to fish or simple grilled meats. The dish can be assembled a day ahead.

SERVES 8

2 medium fennel bulbs, trimmed of feathery leaves and tough stalks and washed (about 2 pounds)
2 tablespoons butter
3 tablespoons unbleached all-purpose flour
1¾ cups milk
¼ teaspoon grated nutmeg
Fine sea salt to taste
½ cup toasted bread crumbs
¼ cup freshly grated Parmigiano-Reggiano cheese

Cut each fennel bulb into quarters. (Save the leaves and stalks for making broth.)

Fill a large pot with water, add 1 tablespoon salt, and bring to a boil. Add the fennel quarters, cover, and cook for about 20 minutes, until a knife can easily be inserted into the fennel. Drain in a colander.

Preheat the oven to 350°F.

In a 1-quart saucepan, melt the butter over medium heat. Add the flour, whisking to form a smooth paste, and cook for about 1 minute. Slowly whisk in the milk and cook, whisking until the sauce begins to thicken. Remove from the heat and stir in the nutmeg and salt.

Spread a thin layer of the sauce in a 12×8-inch casserole dish. Add the fennel, cut sides down, in a single layer. Pour the remaining sauce over the fennel. Sprinkle the bread crumbs and cheese evenly over the top.

Bake uncovered for 25 to 30 minutes, until the sauce and cheese are lightly browned. Serve immediately.

> TIPS: Fennel bulbs often have rust spots on their outer surface. Instead of cutting off and throwing those pieces away, use a vegetable peeler to shave off a thin layer of the outer bulb. This saves wasting the entire piece.
>
> Never throw away the feathery fronds, as they are useful to flavor soups, rub onto meats, and sprinkle over deviled eggs.

## WHITE SAUCE

4 tablespoons (½ stick)
   unsalted butter

¼ cup unbleached all-
   purpose flour

4 cups milk

1 teaspoon salt

¼ teaspoon freshly ground
   nutmeg

## RAGÙ

1 tablespoon butter

1 large carrot, peeled and
   diced

2 celery stalks, diced

1 medium onion, diced

¾ pound ground pork

¼ pound ground beef

¼ pound cooked ham,
   diced

⅔ cup dry white wine

4 large fresh or canned
   plum tomatoes, seeded
   and diced

½ teaspoon salt

Coarsely ground black
   pepper to taste

¼ teaspoon freshly ground
   nutmeg

# La Casseruola di Cipolla da Cannara

## ONION CASSEROLE FROM CANNARA

Many traditional dishes from antipasto to main dishes feature the humble onion as the central ingredient. Cannara, a small town near the ceramic center of Deruta, in Umbria, is known as the onion capital of Italy. So revered are the onions of Cannara that every September a *sagra* (festival) is held called *la festa della cipolla* (the onion festival), where visitors can get their fill of all sorts of tasty onion dishes. My favorite is this exquisite fried onion and ragù casserole laced with white sauce. The dish should be prepared in stages to make the final assembly easy. Make the white and ragù sauces several days ahead and refrigerate them. This outstanding casserole will be a hit on any buffet party table.

SERVES 8 TO 10

To make the white sauce, melt the butter over medium heat in a 2-quart saucepan. Stir in the flour and cook the mixture until it is smooth but not browned. Slowly pour in the milk and continue to cook, stirring frequently, until the sauce thickens enough to coat the back of a spoon. Remove the sauce from the heat and stir in the salt and nutmeg. Cover the pot and set aside, or refrigerate the sauce if you are planning to make the casserole a few days later.

To make the ragù, melt the butter over medium heat in a sauté pan, and cook the carrot, celery, and onion until the mixture is soft. Stir in the pork and beef and brown well. Stir in the ham. Cook for 1 minute longer. Raise the heat to high, pour in the wine, and allow it to evaporate. Stir in the tomatoes, salt, pepper, and nutmeg. Lower the heat and simmer the sauce, covered, for 35 minutes.

To make the filling, put the onion rings in a large paper bag with the flour. Close the bag and shake it to lightly coat the rings.

Heat 1 cup of the vegetable oil in a heavy pot or sauté pan, and when the oil begins to shimmer, add the onions in batches and brown them on both sides. As they brown remove them to paper-towel-lined baking sheets. Add more oil as needed to cook all the onions.

Preheat the oven to 350°F.

Spread ½ cup of the white sauce in the bottom of a 13×8½×2-inch casserole or similar dish.

Spread 2 cups of the ragù over the white sauce. Spread one-third of the onion mixture over the ragù, one-third of the mozzarella cheese over the onions, ½ cup of the white sauce over the mozzarella, and 2 tablespoons of the Parmigiano cheese over the mozzarella. Make two more layers in the same manner. Pour the remaining white sauce over the casserole.

Bake uncovered for 30 to 35 minutes, until it is bubbly and hot.

---

**ONIONS**

2 pounds red onions, cut into ¼-inch-thick rings
5 tablespoons flour
1 to 1½ cups vegetable oil

½ pound mozzarella cheese, diced
6 tablespoons grated Parmigiano-Reggiano cheese

---

> ✻ TIP: Ragù denotes sauces with meat that are cooked for a long time. They differ from place to place. Umbrian ragùs are not as common as other types of sauces; this one is easy to make and is also good on a short cut of pasta such as rigatoni or ziti. Prepare the sauce up to 5 days ahead or make and freeze ahead.

½ pound green beans,
cooked

4 medium all-purpose
potatoes (about 2
pounds), boiled
unpeeled in salted
water

3 eggs

1 tablespoon minced fresh
marjoram

1 small yellow onion,
minced

1 garlic clove, minced

3 tablespoons melted
butter

½ cup grated Parmigiano-
Reggiano cheese

¼ cup milk

Salt to taste

Olive oil for greasing

¾ cup toasted bread
crumbs

# Polpettone di Patata all'Osteria Luchin

## OSTERIA LUCHIN'S POTATO MEAT LOAF

This neat and easy-to-make potato casserole is a favorite of mine from the Osteria Luchin in Liguria, a family-run restaurant where I first sampled it a few years ago. They call it a potato meat loaf. I make it in a cast iron pan, but a regular baking dish will do. Vary the vegetables with asparagùs or small peas.

SERVES 8

Preheat the oven to 350°F.

Mince the green beans and place them in a large bowl. Peel the potatoes and put them through a potato ricer or food mill. Add to the bowl with the string beans. Add the eggs, marjoram, minced onion, garlic, butter, and Parmigiano cheese. Thin with a little milk and season with salt.

Grease a 9-inch cast iron skillet or round baking pan with olive oil and coat with bread crumbs. Press the potato mixture into the pan, and using a fork, create diagonal lines on top. Drizzle with olive oil and bake for 35 to 40 minutes, until hot and crusty. To serve, cut it just as you would a meat loaf.

# Rossolare la Casseruòla di Riso Basmati con le Verdure
## BROWN BASMATI RICE CASSEROLE WITH SAUCY VEGETABLES

Brown basmati rice is a long-grain rice with a fine texture whose nutty flavor complements the pureed vegetables in this casserole, which in turn become a sauce for the rice.

SERVES 6 TO 8

1 cup brown basmati rice
½ teaspoon salt
5 tablespoons unsalted butter
5 medium carrots, peeled and cut into 1-inch chunks
1 medium yellow summer squash, cut in half lengthwise, seeds scooped out and flesh cut into 1-inch chunks
2 large potatoes (about 12 ounces), peeled and cut into 1-inch chunks
½ cup milk
1½ cups grated Parmigiano-Reggiano or pecorino cheese

Preheat the oven to 350°F.

Soak the basmati rice in cold water to cover for 15 minutes. Drain the rice. Bring 2½ cups water to a boil with the salt and 1 tablespoon of the butter. Add the rice and cook until al dente, for 20 to 25 minutes. Drain and set aside.

Place the carrots, squash, and potatoes in a pot and cover with water. Cook until very tender. Drain and transfer to a bowl. Mash with 3 tablespoons of the remaining butter until smooth or use a food processor or immersion blender. Blend in the milk and ½ cup of the cheese. Fold in the rice; taste and add more salt, if necessary.

Spread the mixture in a 9×2-inch round greased pan. Cover the top with the remaining 1 cup of cheese and dot with the remaining 1 tablespoon of butter.

Bake uncovered for 30 to 35 minutes, until the top is nice and crusty. Serve hot.

## Strati di Verdure Miste

## LAYERED MIXED VEGETABLE CASSEROLE

⅓ cup extra virgin olive oil plus extra for drizzling

1 large red onion, thinly sliced

2 large leeks (white bulb only), thinly sliced

Salt to taste

Coarsely ground black pepper to taste

¼ cup white wine vinegar

1 large sweet potato, peeled and thinly sliced

2 large baking potatoes, peeled and thinly sliced

1 large zucchini, stem end trimmed, and thinly sliced

1 summer squash, ends trimmed, and thinly sliced

⅓ cup fresh thyme leaves

1½ cups grated Parmigiano-Reggiano cheese

Vegetables are the foundation of Italian cooking. Just a glance at the Italian food pyramid tells us that vegetables constitute a great part of the Italian diet. This unique vegetable casserole for a crowd is layered with paper-thin slices of zucchini, summer squash, potatoes, and sweet potatoes. It is fun to put together, and a vegetarian's dream. To slice the vegetables, use a mandoline (a French slicing tool), or the slicing hole on a four-sided cheese grater, or the slicing attachment for a food processor.

This casserole is perfect as part of a buffet.

SERVES 8 TO 10

Pour the olive oil into a large skillet or Le Creuset–type casserole dish that is at least 12×2½ inches. Over medium-low heat, cook the onion and leeks until they are soft; season them with salt and pepper as they cook. Cooking them slowly will allow the onions to release their sugar and give a great flavor to the dish. When they are soft, raise the heat to high and pour in the white wine vinegar; cook, stirring occasionally, until the vinegar is nearly evaporated.

Turn off the heat. Spread out the onion mixture evenly in the casserole.

Preheat the oven to 350°F.

Begin making single layers of each vegetable over the onion mixture starting with the sweet potato; sprinkle the layer with salt and pepper, about 1 teaspoon of the thyme, and 2 tablespoons of the cheese. Drizzle a little olive oil evenly over the potato.

Make a second layer like the first, using the baking potato slices. Make a third layer with the zucchini, and a fourth layer with the summer squash.

Repeat the layering so there are eight layers in all. Sprinkle the remaining cheese evenly over the top of the vegetables and drizzle them with olive oil.

Bake covered for 45 minutes; uncover and bake 5 minutes longer.

Serve the casserole by cutting it into wedges or scooping it from the dish.

> ✺ TIP: To prepare the vegetables ahead of time, slice them all (except the baking potatoes) and keep them tightly wrapped separately in plastic wrap. Refrigerate until ready to assemble. Slice the baking potatoes, put them in a bowl, cover with cold water, and refrigerate. When ready to use, drain off the water and pat the potatoes dry.

1 tablespoon unsalted
   butter
1 tablespoon olive oil
1 large leek (white part
   only), finely minced
1 red bell pepper, cut into
   thin strips
2 medium red-skin
   potatoes, cut into ½-
   inch cubes
2 large garlic cloves,
   minced
1 small summer squash,
   grated
1 small zucchini, grated
½ cup stone-ground
   cornmeal
¼ cup unbleached all-
   purpose flour
¼ cup grated Parmigiano-
   Reggiano cheese
2 tablespoons minced
   fresh basil
Salt and freshly ground
   black pepper to taste
1¼ cups milk
2 large eggs
⅓ pound Italian fontina
   cheese, cut into bits

# Polenta con Verdure
## POLENTA AND VEGETABLE CASSEROLE

Polenta, or cooked cornmeal, is used in many ways, such as in this un-usual casserole with a variety of colorful vegetables. Achieve better nu-tritional and taste results by using stone-ground cornmeal. Generic yellow cornmeal is fine, too, if that is all that is available.

SERVES 4 TO 6

Heat the oven to 350° F.

Spray a 9-inch round baking dish with olive oil and set aside.

Heat the butter and olive oil in a large skillet over medium-high heat. Cook the leek, bell pepper, and potatoes for 2 to 3 minutes, stir-ring frequently. Stir in the garlic, squash, and zucchini. Continue cook-ing and stirring until the vegetables begin to soften.

Mix the cornmeal, flour, grated cheese, basil, and salt and pepper together in a large bowl. In a separate bowl, whisk together the milk and eggs.

Whisk the egg mixture into the cornmeal mixture until combined. Stir in the vegetable mixture and combine well. Spread the batter evenly in the baking dish.

Bake for 25 to 30 minutes, until the polenta is almost set but still moist.

Remove from the oven and sprinkle the top with the fontina cheese. Return the casserole to the oven and bake until golden around the edges and the cheese is melted.

Serve hot cut into wedges or scooped from the dish.

# Radicchiella Gratinata
## CRUNCHY BREAD CRUMB–TOPPED DANDELION CASSEROLE

Not too many American cooks take advantage of cooking with dandelions, but Italians seek out this revered vegetable in the spring when the leaves are most tender; they are often boiled and served with nothing more than a drizzle of extra virgin olive oil and a few drops of lemon juice. And as delicious and healthy as that is, this dandelion casserole elevates this bitter chicory to gourmet status. Dandelion greens are easily found in supermarkets. Look for bright green leaves and wash well before using them.

SERVES 4 TO 6

¼ cup pine nuts

1 tablespoon olive oil plus more as needed

½ cup stale bread crumbs

3 pounds dandelion greens, trimmed, well washed, drained, and leaves coarsely chopped

Salt to taste

3 large fresh plum tomatoes, diced

½ cup diced black oil-cured olives

½ cup diced provolone cheese

Preheat the oven to 325°F.

Toast the pine nuts in a 1-quart oven-to-table casserole dish. Transfer them to a small bowl and set aside.

Pour the olive oil in the dish and brown the bread crumbs. Transfer them to a small bowl and set aside.

Pour a thin layer of olive oil in the dish and add the dandelion leaves. Season with salt, then top the leaves with the tomatoes and sprinkle the olives over the tomatoes. Sprinkle the cheese over the olives and bake the dish for 20 minutes. Scatter the pine nuts and bread crumbs over the top and continue baking until the crumbs are crispy, about 5 minutes.

Serve very hot.

---

TIP: To get all the hidden dirt out of dandelion greens, fill a large bowl with cold water and submerge the greens in the bowl for a few minutes. Pour off the water and fill again to repeat the process until no grit remains. Lift the greens from the water and dry them on a clean cloth.

---

3 tablespoons olive oil

1 cup fresh bread crumbs

¼ cup minced fresh oregano or marjoram

Salt to taste

Coarsely ground black pepper to taste

2 pounds plum tomatoes, thinly sliced

2 medium yellow bell peppers, cored, seeded and cut into strips

2 medium eggplants, thinly sliced into rounds

4 medium baking potatoes, peeled and thinly sliced

8 ounces fresh mozzarella cheese, cut into bits

# Tiella di Verdure

## PUGLIESI VEGETABLE CASSEROLE

A typical casserole from the region of Puglia is *tiella di verdure,* a layered vegetable dish that, like the *tiella di cozze* (mussel casserole) on page 15, must contain potatoes according to tradition. It is often served as a first course as an alternative to pasta. The word *tiella* refers to the name of the pan, usually round earthenware, used to cook the casserole.

SERVES 6 TO 8

Preheat the oven to 375°F.

Heat 1 tablespoon of the olive oil in a small sauté pan; stir in the bread crumbs and brown them. Transfer them to a small dish and stir in the oregano. Add salt and pepper; set aside.

Brush a 9½×2-inch casserole dish with the remaining olive oil and arrange layers of tomatoes, bell peppers, eggplant, potatoes, and cheese. Salt and pepper each layer.

Sprinkle the bread crumbs over the top of the casserole and bake for about 1 hour, until the vegetables are tender and the top is crusty. Serve hot or at room temperature.

# Tortiera di Patate, Pomodori e Cipolle

## POTATO, TOMATO, AND ONION CASSEROLE

Here is a simple casserole made with staple ingredients that just about everyone has: potatoes, onions, and tomatoes. It is especially good when ripe garden tomatoes are in season.

SERVES 4 TO 6

2 tablespoons olive oil

2 large russet or Yukon Gold potatoes, peeled and cut into thin rounds

6 large fresh plum or beefsteak tomatoes, thinly sliced

2 medium red onions, sliced into thin rounds

Salt to taste

1 cup grated pecorino cheese

2 tablespoons minced fresh marjoram leaves

½ cup dry white wine such as Pinot Grigio

Preheat the oven to 375°F.

Brush the olive oil in a 9 × 12-inch casserole dish. Starting with the potatoes, make three alternating layers of potatoes, tomatoes, and onions. Sprinkle each layer with salt and ⅓ cup of the cheese and marjoram.

Pour the wine carefully into the dish at one side. Cover the dish with aluminum foil and bake for 25 to 30 minutes. Uncover the dish and continue baking until the top is nicely browned.

# Tortino di Carciofi

## SARDINIAN ARTICHOKE CASSEROLE

Two 9-ounce packages frozen artichoke hearts, thawed and drained

4 large eggs

¼ cup extra virgin olive oil

3 tablespoons chopped fresh Italian parsley

½ cup grated pecorino or Parmigiano-Reggiano cheese

Juice of 1 lemon

Sea salt and freshly ground black pepper to taste

½ cup toasted bread crumbs

3 fresh plum tomatoes, thinly sliced

Glorious artichokes, both thornless and thorny types, grow on the island of Sardinia, and are tender enough to be eaten raw. Oh, to be that *fortunata* here! But you can make this wonderful and quick artichoke casserole with frozen artichoke hearts if you do not want to bother with prepping the fresh Globe variety available in supermarkets.

SERVES 4 TO 6

Cut the artichoke hearts into thin slices and set aside.

Whisk together the eggs and olive oil in a bowl. Stir in the parsley, cheese, lemon juice, and salt and pepper.

Preheat the oven to 325°F.

Lightly grease a 9-inch casserole dish and sprinkle in ¼ cup of the bread crumbs. Spread the artichoke hearts evenly over the bread crumbs, then overlap the tomato slices over the artichokes.

Pour the egg mixture evenly over the tomatoes. Sprinkle the top with the remaining bread crumbs. Bake uncovered for 30 to 40 minutes, or until the top is nicely browned. Serve hot.

# Zucchine e Pomodori
## ZUCCHINI AND TOMATO CASSEROLE

This easy-to-put-together zucchini and tomato casserole can also do duty as an antipasto, light lunch, or side to a meat, fish, or poultry course. It is the perfect summer dish when tomatoes and zucchini are at their peak of freshness.

SERVES 8

Preheat the oven to 350°F.

Melt the butter over medium heat in a nonstick sauté pan and brown the bread triangles on both sides. Set aside to cool.

Heat 1 tablespoon of the oil in the same pan; stir in the bread crumbs and brown them in the oil. Transfer the crumbs to a small bowl; stir in the oregano and salt and pepper. Set the mixture aside.

Lightly coat a 9×12×2-inch baking dish with 1 tablespoon of the remaining olive oil. Make a layer of tomatoes in the base of the dish and sprinkle them with a little salt and pepper. Make a layer of zucchini over the tomatoes. Sprinkle the zucchini with half the cheese. Make two more layers each of tomatoes, zucchini, and salt and pepper. Make a final layer of zucchini, the remaining cheese, and tomato slices. Place the bread triangles in a layer over the tomatoes. Drizzle with the remaining 1 tablespoon olive oil.

Cover the baking pan with foil and bake for 20 minutes. Remove the foil and bake for an additional 30 minutes. Five minutes before the dish is done, sprinkle the bread crumb and oregano mixture evenly over the top. Serve hot or at room temperature.

2 tablespoons unsalted butter
4 slices country-style bread, crusts trimmed and each slice cut into 4 triangles
3 tablespoons olive oil
½ cup fresh bread crumbs
1¼ teaspoons dried oregano
Sea salt to taste
Coarsely ground black pepper to taste
4 or 5 large plum tomatoes, peeled and sliced into thin rounds
2 medium zucchini, sliced into thin rounds
½ pound Italian fontina cheese, cut into small pieces

½ cup olive oil
1 large onion, diced
1 medium fennel bulb, trimmed of feathery leaves and tough stalks and diced
5 plum tomatoes, peeled, seeded, and pureed
1¾ pounds red-skin potatoes, peeled and diced
1 pound eggplant, peeled and diced
1 pound zucchini, diced
Fine sea salt to taste
Coarsely ground black pepper to taste
1 large yellow bell pepper, cored, seeded, and cut into thin strips
½ cup packed fresh basil leaves, chopped

# Ciambotta
## VEGETABLE STEW

From the region of Calabria in the south comes a classic *ciambotta* (meaning all mixed up), a hearty vegetable stew of eggplant, zucchini, tomatoes, fennel, potatoes, onions, and peppers. Use your imagination for other veggie combinations. Slow cooking blends the flavors and prevents the vegetables from losing their shape.

SERVES 8 TO 10

Heat the olive oil in a Dutch oven over medium heat. Add the onion and sauté until soft. Add the fennel and continue cooking until it is soft. Add the tomatoes, potatoes, eggplant, zucchini, ½ cup water, and salt and pepper and stir well. Cover and cook over low heat for 20 minutes.

Add the pepper strips and cook for about 10 minutes more, until the vegetables are tender but not mushy. Stir in the basil.

> TIP: Ciambotta can also serve as a sauce for pasta or a topping for grilled polenta, or can be combined with rice.

# Zuppa di Val d'Aosta
## CABBAGE CASSEROLE FROM THE VAL D'AOSTA

From the Val d'Aosta in northern Italy comes this thick, savory Savoy cabbage soup that could double as a casserole. The soup is layered between slices of coarse stale rye bread, which gives this casserole great character even though the ingredients are humble at best.

SERVES UP TO 6

1 large head savoy cabbage, cored and coarsely chopped
4 strips bacon, diced
1 pound loaf stale coarse rye bread, sliced thinly and toasted
3 tablespoons fresh savory or marjoram
½ pound Italian fontina cheese, cut into small pieces
6 tablespoons unsalted butter
4 cups beef broth
Salt to taste

Preheat the oven to 300°F.

Simmer the cabbage with the bacon and just a couple of tablespoons of water in a nonaluminum 3½-quart stovetop-to-oven casserole dish with a lid. Cook until the cabbage wilts down. Transfer it to a bowl.

Wipe out the casserole and line it with a layer of the toasted bread slices. Top with a layer of cabbage and sprinkle on some of the herbs and some of the cheese. Dot with butter.

Continue making layers until the cabbage and bread are used up. End with a layer of bread topped with a layer of cheese.

Pour the meat broth around the sides of the casserole.

Bake covered for 45 minutes. Uncover and bake 15 minutes longer.

# Tutte Frutte
## *Casseroles*

Buccellato alle Fragole e
Mascarpone
(Buccellato with Strawberries and
Mascarpone)

Budino di Panettone e Fichi
Secchi
(Panettone and Dried Fig Bread
Pudding)

Budino di Pane e Mele con la
Salsa di Caramel
(Apple Bread Pudding with Caramel
Sauce)

Budino di Riso con Ciliegie
(Baked Rice and Cherry Casserole)

Fichi Secchi con Finocchio,
Cipolline, e Vino
(Dried Figs with Fennel, Onions,
and Wine)

Pesche e Panna
(Peaches and Cream)

Tutte Frutte Miste in Vino
Rosso
(Mixed Fruit Casserole in Red Wine)

Zuccotto

FRUIT ON ITS OWN IS THE QUINTESSENTIAL DESSERT for all Italians but that is not to say that it cannot be transformed into some very tasty fruit and bread "casseroles," some of which are baked and served warm, while others are meant to be served cold or at room temperature, such as the strawberry "lasagne" on page 131. When making fruit casseroles, use any type of sweet bread, like *panettone*, fresh or stale, or *buccellatto*, a yeast based raisin bread; in their place, substitute cinnamon bread, coffee cakes, and pound cake. Don't use sweet breads or cakes that do not have a tight crumb like angel food cake, since they tend to break apart when moistened.

Some of the best fruits for casseroles are apples, pears, apricots, peaches, and fresh cherries, since they hold up well in cooking; but delicate fruits like blueberries and raspberries are also good choices; just remember to handle them gingerly and mix them in lightly.

For baked casseroles, pick fruits that are in season, not overly ripe, and yield to slight pressure when pressed with your finger.

Fruit juices, wine, and liqueurs are perfect for giving added flavor and providing moisture.

# Buccellato alle Fragole e Mascarpone

## BUCCELLATO WITH STRAWBERRIES AND MASCARPONE

Let's just say that you have too much of a good *buccellato* on hand. What to do? This sweet, yeasted bread makes a sensational layered dessert casserole when slices are soaked in a strawberry wine sauce. Instead of baking it, refrigerate it, then cut it like a layered lasagne. If you don't have a *buccellato,* a good loaf of challah is a perfect and delicious substitute. *Fantastico!*

SERVES 8

1 pound ripe strawberries, stemmed and cut into slices
⅓ cup sugar
Juice of 1 large lemon
5 cups dry red wine
24 slices of buccellato or enough to fill a 9×13-inch glass pan to make 3 layers
1 cup whipping cream
¼ cup mascarpone or cream cheese at room temperature
2 tablespoons confectioners' sugar
Mint leaves for garnish

Mash the berries in a large bowl with a fork. Stir in the sugar and lemon juice. Pour in the wine and mix well. Cover the bowl and refrigerate the mixture for 3 hours.

Line a 9×13-inch pan with eight slices buccellato, trimming them if necessary to fit the pan. Cover the slices with some of the wine sauce. Keep making two more alternating layers of bread and sauce, ending with the sauce mixture on top. Cover the pan and refrigerate for several hours to allow the bread to absorb all the liquid.

Whip the cream with the mascarpone or cream cheese and the sugar until stiff.

When ready to serve cut the buccellato into serving pieces like lasagne. Place them on individual dessert dishes and top with some of the whipped cream. Add mint leaves for garnish and serve.

## Budino di Panettone e Fichi Secchi
### PANETTONE AND DRIED FIG BREAD PUDDING

4 cups 1-inch pieces
    panettone or other
    sweet bread
1 cup sweet Marsala wine
10 dried Calamyrna figs,
    stemmed and cut into
    small pieces
4 cups milk
½ cup light cream
½ teaspoon ground
    cinnamon
¼ teaspoon freshly grated
    nutmeg
1 teaspoon salt
2 tablespoons grated
    orange zest
2 tablespoons grated
    lemon zest
4 large eggs, separated
⅓ cup sugar
Whipped cream or vanilla
    gelato

*Panettone* is a classic sweet yeast bread that Italians give as gifts at Christmastime, but it is readily available year-round. Leftover panettone makes a great bread pudding when combined with dried figs. No panettone? Other types of sweet breads can also be used, like brioche or cinnamon or raisin bread.

SERVES 8 TO 10

Preheat the oven to 325°F.

Butter a 9 × 12-inch casserole dish.

Place the bread in a large bowl. Add the wine and toss until the bread is evenly moistened. Set aside.

Put the figs into a small bowl and pour hot water over them; allow the figs to soak for 10 minutes, then drain and set aside.

Bring the milk and cream to a boil in a large saucepan. Remove from the heat and stir in the cinnamon, nutmeg, salt, and orange and lemon zests.

Whisk the egg yolks in a large bowl until light and fluffy. Whisk in the milk mixture.

Beat the egg whites in a separate bowl with a handheld mixer until they are foamy. Sprinkle in the sugar and beat the whites until soft peaks are formed. Fold the white mixture into the egg yolk mixture. Fold in the bread pieces and the figs.

Pour into the casserole. Place the casserole in a large pan like a roasting pan and pour hot water into the roasting pan until it reaches halfway up the sides of the casserole.

Bake the budino until a knife blade inserted in the center is just slightly wet. This may take between 1½ and 2 hours.

Remove the casserole from the roasting pan and wipe the bottom with a towel.

Serve the budino warm with a garnish of whipped cream or a small scoop of vanilla gelato.

# Budino di Pane e Mele con la Salsa di Caramel
## APPLE BREAD PUDDING WITH CARAMEL SAUCE

Any leftover sweet bread like *panettone* or *ciambelle*, or even raisin bread, is a good candidate for this delicious bread pudding with apples and caramel sauce. It is baked in a *bagnomaria* (water bath), which gives the pudding even heat and provides a wonderful textural taste.

SERVES 6 TO 8

½ cup raisins, dried cranberries, or dried cherries
⅓ cup brandy
12 slices sweet bread, torn into 1-inch pieces
1½ cups light cream
1⅓ cups sugar
¼ teaspoon grated nutmeg
3 large eggs
½ teaspoon salt
3 tablespoons melted butter
4 Golden Delicious apples, cored, peeled, and thinly sliced

In a small bowl, soak the raisins in the brandy for 30 minutes.

Place the bread pieces in a rectangular casserole dish and pour the cream over it. Set aside.

In a large bowl, whisk ½ cup of the sugar with the nutmeg, eggs, salt, and butter until well blended. Drain the raisins and add to the sugar mixture along with 2 tablespoons of the brandy. Add the apple slices and soaked bread slices. Combine well. Set aside.

Preheat the oven to 350°F.

In a saucepan set over medium-high heat, combine the remaining sugar and ⅓ cup water. Let the sugar dissolve completely, then boil until it darkens to a caramel color. Immediately pour it into an 9½ × 2½ deep ring mold and swirl to coat the bottom of the mold. Be careful not to hold the mold by the bottom or you may burn your hand. Hold it by the rim.

Pour the apple bread mixture into the mold, spreading and packing it evenly with a wooden spoon.

Place the mold in a baking pan and pour in enough boiling water around the outside of the mold to come 1½ inches up the sides.

Carefully transfer the pan to the oven and bake for 45 minutes or until a cake tester inserted in the middle comes out still slightly damp.

Remove the mold from the pan and allow it to cool for a few minutes. Carefully place a round rimmed serving dish or platter larger than the mold over the top of the mold and invert it.

Shake to release the pudding and the sauce. Cut into wedges and serve warm.

# Budino di Riso con Ciliegie
## BAKED RICE AND CHERRY CASSEROLE

1 cup half-and-half or nonfat half-and-half

1¼ cups whole or low-fat milk

½ cup arborio or carnaroli rice

¼ teaspoon sea salt

½-inch piece vanilla bean, split lengthwise

½ cup sugar

3 large eggs, slightly beaten

Grated zest of 1 lemon

⅛ teaspoon cinnamon

1 cup diced pitted Bing cherries

1 tablespoon melted butter

1 cup sliced almonds

### CHERRY SAUCE

1 tablespoon butter, cut into bits

¼ cup sugar

1 cup pitted Bing cherries, cut in half

2 tablespoons amaretto liqueur

A *budino di riso* is a rice pudding, and the best are made with arborio or carnaroli rice, a starchy rice used to make risotto. In this version of the classic budino, the rice is baked in a *bagnomaria* (water bath), which provides even heat and results in a light and creamy texture. Start using your imagination by adding other ingredients such as dried or fresh fruits, or fruits and nuts, and transform the budino into a delightful rice casserole.

SERVES 6

Combine the half-and-half, milk, rice, and salt in a 2-quart saucepan. Bring to a boil, then reduce the heat to a simmer. Scrape the seeds from the vanilla bean into the rice mixture, then add the vanilla bean piece. Cover the pot and cook until most of the liquid is absorbed. The rice should look soupy. This should take 25 to 30 minutes. Remove and rinse the vanilla bean and save for another use. Transfer the mixture to a bowl. Stir in the sugar and let the mixture cool.

Preheat the oven to 325°F.

Combine the eggs, lemon zest, and cinnamon in a small bowl. Stir the mixture into the cooled rice. Gently fold in the diced cherries.

Brush a 1½- to 2-quart casserole dish with the melted butter and spoon the rice mixture into the pan. Place the casserole in a larger pan.

Slowly pour boiling water along the sides of the larger pan so it comes halfway up the sides of the casserole.

Bake for 20 minutes; sprinkle the almonds evenly over the top, and continue baking for an additional 10 to 15 minutes, until a knife inserted in the center comes out clean but the pudding still jiggles when shaken. Remove from the oven and allow to cool for about 15 minutes.

To make the sauce, melt the butter in a saucepan over medium heat and stir in the sugar. Cook until the sugar dissolves. Stir in the cherries and continue cooking until the cherries are glazed. Raise the heat to medium-high and stir in the amaretto. Cook for 1 minute. Transfer the sauce to a small bowl and allow it to cool to room temperature.

Scoop the rice pudding from the casserole into individual dessert dishes and drizzle some of the cherry sauce over the top.

CIAO ITALIA SLOW AND EASY

# Fichi Secchi con Finocchio, Cipolline e Vino

## DRIED FIGS WITH FENNEL, ONIONS, AND WINE

It has been said that the Italians could exist on figs alone. Figs (fichi) have always been a quintessential part of Italian cooking, whether served fresh alone, or as an accompaniment to the classic prosciutto di Parma. When fresh figs are not in season, dried figs take their place. In this contemporary side dish, dried figs are paired with fennel, small flat onions called cipolline, wine, and balsamic vinegar. Slow-cooked together, the combination creates a sweet, caramelized taste that is a refreshing choice for roast turkey, pork chops, capon, or chicken. So hold the cranberry sauce and try it at your next holiday dinner. Substitute shallots if cipolline onions are not available.

SERVES 6 TO 8

2 tablespoons olive oil
10 small (1 inch in diameter) cippoline onions or shallots, halved
1 medium fennel bulb (white part only), thinly sliced
10 dried figs, stemmed and cut in half lengthwise
½ cup dry red wine
¼ teaspoon ground cinnamon
¼ teaspoon ground cloves
Grated zest of 1 large orange
Salt to taste
2 tablespoons commercial balsamic vinegar

Preheat the oven to 325°F.

Heat the olive oil in a medium oven-to-table casserole dish. Stir in the cipolline and cook them until they begin to soften and look glazed. Stir in the fennel and cook until the fennel begins to soften. Off the heat scatter the figs on top of the cippoline mixture.

Combine the wine, cinnamon, cloves, orange zest, and salt in a small bowl. Pour the mixture over the figs.

Cover the dish with a lid or heavy-duty aluminum foil and bake for 30 to 35 minutes. Uncover the dish and spoon the juices over the fig mixture. Sprinkle the dish with balsamic vinegar and continue to bake uncovered for an additional 5 minutes.

Serve with poultry, fish, or pork.

> TIPS: Onions, shallots, and garlic are best stored in a cool, dark area to prevent sprouting, and used within a week of purchase.
>
> Citrus fruits such as oranges and lemons will zest better if they are at room temperature.

20 amaretti cookies, crushed to a fine consistency

8 tablespoons melted and cooled butter

4 large white peaches, peeled, pitted, and cut into thin slices

2 large white nectarines, peeled, pitted, and cut into thin slices

Juice of 1 large lemon

2 cups heavy whipping cream

⅓ cup sugar

¼ teaspoon almond extract

# Pesche e Panna
## PEACHES AND CREAM

This refreshing no-bake casserole is one of my favorite summertime desserts and it all has to do with heavenly white peaches, which the Italians call *pesca bianca*. For my money, their white flesh and perfumed taste can't be beat. I like to mix them with white nectarines and fold them into slightly sweetened whipped cream. The crunch comes from amaretti di Saronno, those tiny almond cookies from northern Italy.

SERVES 6

Combine the amaretti crumbs in a bowl with the melted butter and mix well to combine. Press half the cookies into an 8-inch-square pan and refrigerate. Set the rest aside.

Combine the peaches and nectarines in a separate bowl with the lemon juice and set aside.

Whip the cream in a large bowl in an electric mixer on high speed until stiff; stir in the sugar and the almond extract.

Drain the peaches and nectarines in a colander and fold into the whipped cream. Spread the mixture evenly and carefully over the amaretti.

Sprinkle the remaining amaretti over the top.

Refrigerate for at least 2 hours or overnight.

Scoop to serve or cut into squares.

> TIP: Amaretti di Saronno work best in this recipe; find them in Italian specialty stores, online, or in grocery stores. Substitute vanilla wafer cookies if amaretti are unavailable.

# Tutte Frutte Miste in Vino Rosso

## MIXED FRUIT CASSEROLE IN RED WINE

Just combine your favorite fruits and slowly cook them in wine or citrus for the easiest dessert casseroles, then top them with sweetened mascarpone cheese or a scoop of gelato.

SERVES 4

Preheat the oven to 325°F.

Squeeze the juice from one orange and set aside. Peel the other orange, removing as much of the pith as possible, and cut it into thin slices. Place the slices in a bowl. Add the peaches or nectarines, pear, figs, and apple to the bowl with the orange slices.

Sprinkle the flour over the fruit and mix gently with a spoon. Transfer the fruit to a 9-inch casserole dish with a lid.

In a small bowl combine the sugar, wine, and reserved orange juice. Pour over the fruit.

Bake covered for 45 minutes. Remove the casserole from the oven and allow it to cool to room temperature.

To serve, fill each of four footed dessert goblets or wineglasses with some of the fruit and syrup. Place a dollop of mascarpone cheese or gelato over the top of each goblet and garnish with mint leaves.

2 blood oranges or navel oranges
2 white peaches or nectarines, peeled, pitted, and thinly sliced
1 Bosc pear, peeled, cored, and thinly sliced
4 fresh figs, stemmed and cut in half
1 large Yellow Delicious apple, peeled, cored, and thinly sliced
2 tablespoons unbleached all-purpose flour
⅓ cup brown sugar
1 cup red wine
Mascarpone cheese or vanilla gelato
Mint leaves for garnish

> TIP: Lemon or orange sorbet is also good in place of the gelato.

# Zuccotto

## PASTRY CREAM
2 cups whole milk
1 tablespoon vanilla
    extract
4 large egg yolks
¼ cup unbleached all-
    purpose flour
½ cup granulated sugar

## CAKE
2 tablespoons brandy
1 tablespoon granulated
    sugar
¾ pound (about 30)
    ladyfingers
1¾ cups heavy cream,
    whipped to firm peaks
¾ cup sliced strawberries
8 ounces bittersweet
    chocolate, chopped
    medium fine, plus extra
    chocolate for making
    curls
Confectioners' sugar for
    sprinkling

*Zuccotto* is the name given to a molded and richly layered pastry cream–filled dessert that is said to resemble the dome of Florence's great cathedral. And as the cathedral was built in stages, so too can zuccotto be made. Make the pastry cream and chop the chocolate several days ahead. Once the zuccotto is assembled, it will need to be refrigerated overnight before the finishing touches of whipped cream and chocolate curls are added. Be sure to use good quality, hard Italian ladyfingers, not the spongy type found in grocery stores. Most Italian specialty stores carry them.

SERVES 10

Bring the milk to a boil in a saucepan over medium heat. Remove the pan from the heat and stir in the vanilla. Set aside to cool slightly.

In the top of a double boiler off the heat, whisk the egg yolks. Slowly whisk in the flour, then the milk. Return the double boiler to the heat and cook, stirring constantly with a wooden spoon until the cream thickens and coats the spoon. Stir in the sugar. Pour the pastry cream into a bowl and cover with a piece of buttered wax paper, pressing it against the surface of the cream. Refrigerate overnight or several days ahead of assembling the cake.

For the cake, line an 8¾ by 4¼-inch glass bowl with plastic wrap, allowing several inches to hang over the sides of the bowl. Fill a spritzer with the brandy, 1 teaspoon water, and sugar and use it to spritz the ladyfingers as you construct the cake.

Start lining the sides of the bowl with ladyfingers, standing them up vertically and making sure the tops of the ladyfingers are even with the rim of the bowl. If they are not, trim them with a knife. Use a couple of broken ladyfingers to line the bottom of the bowl.

Carefully spread about ⅓ cup of pastry cream over the ladyfingers in the bottom of the bowl. Spread about 3 tablespoons of whipped cream over the pastry cream. Arrange a layer of ladyfingers over the whipped cream and spritz with the brandy mixture. Spread about

⅓ cup of the pastry cream over the ladyfingers. Arrange the strawberries over the pastry cream, pressing them gently into the cream. Sprinkle half of the chocolate over the strawberries.

Cover the chocolate with another layer of ladyfingers and spritz with the brandy mixture. Spread the remaining pastry cream over the ladyfingers and sprinkle the remaining chocolate over the pastry cream. Spread the remaining whipped cream over the chocolate.

Add a final layer of ladyfingers, covering the filling completely, and spritz again with the brandy mixture. Bring the overhanging edges of the plastic wrap up over the top of the cake, pressing down on the cake gently with your hand. Refrigerate overnight.

To unmold, unwrap the top of the cake. Place a serving dish over the top and invert the mold. Carefully remove the plastic wrap from the cake. Sprinkle the cake top with confectioners' sugar or remaining whipped cream to serve. Or whip additional cream and use a pastry bag with a star tip to make a decorative border around the base and top of the cake. Use a vegetable peeler to make chocolate curls from a block of chocolate and sprinkle the curls over the cream border. Serve immediately.

# INDEX